COOKING

Made Easy

Quick, Delicious Meals
for Your Healthy Zone Lifestyle

GLORIA BAKST

WITH **MARY GOODBODY**

McGraw·Hill

New York   Chicago   San Francisco   Lisbon   London   Madrid   Mexico City
Milan   New Delhi   San Juan   Seoul   Singapore   Sydney   Toronto

Library of Congress Cataloging-in-Publication Data

Bakst, Gloria.
    ZonePerfect cooking make easy : quick, delicious meals for your healthy zone
lifestyle / by Gloria Bakst, with Mary Goodbody.
        p.   cm.
    ISBN 0-07-145790-9
        1. Reducing diets—Recipes.   2. Nutrition.   I. Goodbody, Mary.   II. Title.
    III. Title: ZonePerfect cooking make easy.

    RM222.2.B348   2006
    641.5'63—dc22   2006012761

1 2 3 4 5 6 7 8 9 0   FGR/FGR   0 9 8 7 6

ISBN-13: 978-0-07-145790-3
ISBN-10:   0-07-145790-9

Featured on the cover: Roasted Red Snapper with Vegetables (page 133)

Interior design by Nick Panos and Pam Juarez

McGraw-Hill books are available at special quantity discounts to use as premiums and
sales promotions, or for use in corporate training programs. For more information, please
write to the Director of Special Sales, Professional Publishing, McGraw-Hill, Two Penn
Plaza, New York, NY 10121-2298. Or contact your local bookstore.

The information contained in this book is intended to provide helpful and informative
material on the subject addressed. It is not intended to serve as a replacement for
professional medical advice. Any use of the information in this book is at the reader's
discretion. The author and publisher specifically disclaim any and all liability arising
directly or indirectly from the use or application of any information contained in this book.
A health care professional should be consulted regarding your specific situation.

This book is printed on acid-free paper.

To my mom, with love, a fabulous cook who taught me how to cook and who collaborated with me on many of the recipes in this book. To my dad, with love, who knows how to eat and appreciates good food.

Contents

*A*cknowledgments

ZonePerfect Cooking Made Easy is a dream come true. For the last twenty years, I have been cooking and creating healthful recipes. Ten years ago, when I committed to the Zone, I adapted my earlier recipes to work in the Zone, even while I developed new ones. As I worked, I kept the hope alive that I would one day publish a cookbook to showcase these nutritious, fast, user-friendly, and, most important, delicious and healthful recipes and to explain how easy it is to live in the Zone. This exuberant lifestyle supports your body and your mind so that you feel your very best at all times.

I want to thank the many people who made this book a reality. First, a big thanks to the folks at ZonePerfect: Paul Pruett, former chief operating officer, who is the greatest boss ever and who was so encouraging and helpful when the book was just getting off the ground; Mark Gorman, former president of the Ross Products division; Mike Ferry, divisional vice president of Ross Products/Abbott Laboratories, for keeping things moving; Mary Drennan, marketing director; and Christopher Calamari, for all their support.

Thanks to my friends Rux Martin and Barry Estabrook for giving me the confidence to "Go for it!"

I want to thank my valued, hardworking literary agent, Jane Dystel, to whom I am deeply grateful. I also want to thank the team at Dystel & Goderich Literary Management, who worked together to get this book to McGraw-Hill.

My deepest gratitude goes to Judith McCarthy, my editor at McGraw-Hill, who is such a delight to work with and is so accommodating.

I want to thank my coauthor, Mary Goodbody, who is simply the most delicious food writer, tremendously supportive, and a source of much information, and who now is my friend.

My mother and father instilled in me a love for and playful attitude toward food, something I have found to be priceless. My mom is a valuable and reliable resource for recipes and knowledge, and a number of the recipes in this book are adapted from hers.

Thanks to Deborah Callan for testing many of the recipes so professionally. I want to thank my sister Audrey Koren and my cousin Linda Paul for tasting and testing recipes, too. I am indebted to author Corinne T. Netzer, whose *Complete Book of Food Counts* (Dell Publishing, 2000) was enormously helpful in figuring the nutritional analyses with the recipes. I would have been lost without my brother-in-law, Woody Bakst, who made countless trips to Whole Foods Market for ingredients and also helped with nutritional calculations. Thanks, Woody! I would like to thank Joyce Colohan and Dance Energy for keeping me moving.

Heartfelt thanks go to my wonderful kids, Justin, Hayley, and Kerin, for being so supportive as I conceptualized and then wrote this book—and for being so open to trying new dishes.

I owe an enormous debt of gratitude to my dear friends who have been there for me through challenging times and have rejoiced with me during the triumphs: Betsy Ostroff and David Weiss; Amy Nechtem and Eric Smith; Gerdy Weiss; Kate and Rick Moltz; Susan and Larry Goldberg; and Amy and Mark Farber. You have been a source of support and pleasure, and I count you as extended family of the best sort.

Most important, I want to thank my husband, Bobby, whose goal in life seems to be to make me happy, and who always succeeds. He was instrumental in making this book happen, and absolutely none of it would have been possible without him. He is the most supportive, adoring man I know, and I love him dearly.

Finally, thank you to all the loyal Zone followers. I hope you get as much from this book as I have gotten from meeting and knowing you over the years.

*I*ntroduction

Welcome to the ZonePerfect World

I wasn't born in the Zone! Truth be told, it took a good number of years before I discovered this life-affirming plan that has changed my life and given me such enormous peace of mind.

My story is not one of extremes. I was never a particularly poor eater, excessively overweight, or someone who loaded up on "bad" foods such as burgers, fries, and buttery pastas. On the contrary, before I landed in the Zone, I was eating what most people would consider a healthful diet. But I didn't feel quite right. I was often anxious and irritable, lacked energy, and noticed that my sleep patterns went from restless to wide awake and back again.

I happened to read about the Zone and its belief in hormonal balance achieved by a good, rounded diet of balanced meals. I was intrigued. The diet was one thing, but the overall approach to a new way of living was most appealing. I was not interested in a weight-loss diet but was attracted to the idea of a lifestyle sea change that would enable me to live more fully.

When I read about carbohydrate overloading and how it contributes to carbo cravings only a few hours after a meal, I quickly recognized a familiar symptom. In those days, I frequently felt light-headed after working out and couldn't wait to get home and stuff carbs into my mouth. How could this be bad for me? I craved "good carbs" such as brown rice, wheat crackers, and whole wheat bread. I later discovered I was addicted to brown rice, of all things.

Most people are addicted to sugar. Either way, it's too many simple carbohydrates wreaking havoc on our systems.

I later learned that carb overload is a classic mistake a lot of people make and also that it was a sign that I was hypoglycemic, which is not the case for everyone. Now that I am living in the Zone, my hypoglycemia is under control and I feel terrific!

How the Zone Works

Its bedrock foundation makes the Zone the ideal diet for anyone who has tried others and would like to make a lifelong change. Whether you have been on the Atkins or the South Beach diets, or have tried to shed pounds with Jenny Craig or Weight Watchers, the Zone way of life is for you. The key phrase is "way of life." Living and eating in the Zone is a life choice, not only for those wanting to lose weight, but for anyone who wants to live a healthy, happy life.

When you eat and live in the Zone, every meal comprises a sensible balance of 40 percent carbohydrates, 30 percent protein, and 30 percent fat. This is the 40-30-30 approach you may already associate with the Zone.

Being in the Zone means eating three meals a day and two snacks. You don't count calories, and you never skip a meal. You practice sensible portion control and pay attention to what you eat, which means staying away from sugar; limiting unfavorable carbohydrates such as bread, pasta, rice, and potatoes; and avoiding animal fats as much as possible.

The 40-30-30 balance maintains the body so that it is in perfect hormonal equilibrium. When you achieve this stability, everything works right. And when everything works right, you feel great.

How This Book Works

If you have read about the Zone elsewhere, you may be surprised to learn that I don't rely on the block system. Instead, I measure grams of carbohydrates, protein, and fat. I find this easier for everyday use and handy when reading the nutrition labels on packages in the supermarket. A single, whole block, as used by other proponents of the Zone, contains 9 grams of carbohydrates, 7 grams of protein, and 3 grams of fat. I broke out of this constraint but rely on the same principles and ratios. My method is a simplified one designed to make sense to even the most harried home cook.

When I calculated grams for my recipes, I was as accurate as possible, but because cooking is not an exact science, I could be off by a gram here and there. This is the nature of nutritional analyses: at best they are very good estimates. Use them as guides as you enter the Zone. Keep in mind, too, that when I figured the analyses, I did not count any garnishes or optional ingredients. Rarely do these add anything but flavor and color. Additionally, most of the marinades I use are so thin that they slide right off the food and so I divide the nutritional amounts in half.

Finally, when I calculated the fat for dishes that included lean protein (fish, chicken, and turkey), I did not count the 1.5 grams of fat naturally present in every ounce of *all* lean protein. When I calculated the carbohydrates, I took into account the amount of fiber in the food, because you subtract the total number of fiber grams from the total number of carbohydrates. Foods high in fiber, such as garbanzo beans and lentils, may be high in carbs, too, but the fiber automatically reduces the carbohydrates that are actually absorbed into the body. As is standard practice, I considered this when I figured the nutritional analysis, and so you see the lowered (and correct) carbohydrate count.

Once you have gotten used to the 40-30-30 ratio, you will know when you are eating correctly. You will feel great and want to stay in the Zone to maintain this sense of well-being. Yet it's comforting to know that when you've made one too many exceptions or gotten a little lazy, you can quickly return to counting grams and get back on track. For more on this and some help "eyeballing" your food, turn to page 7.

Some people are surprised that there is as much fat as there is in the Zone diet. Fat is essential to maintain a healthful hormonal balance. All protein contains fat and nearly all my recipes contain small amounts of added fat, such as olive oil. I don't think food tastes as good if it's totally fat-free, and there's no reason to eliminate all fat. And fat burns fat, helping you feel sated. So, keep some fat—you want to enjoy your meals!

The notable exception to this rule is trans (hydrogenated) fats. These are never good for you. While monounsaturated fats (such as olive oil, rapeseed oil, almonds, Brazil nuts, cashews, and avocados), and polyunsaturated fats (such as soy, safflower, and corn oils), are considered "good fats," and saturated fats, found in animal products, are not good for you and so should be limited, trans fats are just plain bad for you. Trans fats are found primarily in processed foods, margarine, and fried foods. Food companies like them because they extend shelf life, but they are associated with cardiac disease, diabetes, and even some cancers. Read food labels and stay away from the words "partially hydrogenated," which indicate the presence of trans fats.

Finally, keep in mind that the Zone is not a weight-loss diet that you dip into when you want to shed pounds. It's an eating system and philosophy that will stay with you forever and help you lead a healthier, happier, more active life.

Join Me in the Zone

Whether you want to drop pounds, develop a healthful eating plan, increase your energy, improve your general health, or accomplish all four, the Zone is for you. I firmly believe this, and I am thrilled you are going to join me in the Zone.

Here is what I have experienced and believe you can look forward to:

- You will look better because losing weight will be practically effortless.
- You will feel confident because maintaining your weight will be easy.
- You will have more energy to accomplish daily tasks.

- You will look forward to exercising and being active.
- You will have more mental agility.
- You will sleep much, much better.
- You will catch fewer colds and flu-like viruses.
- You will notice a decrease of everyday aches and pains.
- You will enjoy thinking about your next meal but won't feel hungry.
- You will add delicious recipes to your regular repertoire.
- Your skin will glow, your hair will shine, and your nails won't split or break.

Sounds great! What are you waiting for? With this book in hand, you can enter the Zone easily and happily. All my recipes are Zone friendly and use Zone-favorable foods, and all are developed with busy families in mind. Plus, I have peppered the book with tips for living, cooking, and shopping in the Zone that are designed to give even the most skeptical home cook the confidence to try.

As the working mother of two children and wife of a busy husband, I know only too well how little time anyone has and how precious are our few moments at the supper table. Because of this, I have worked hard to make entering the Zone accessible and family oriented. There are very few odd or hard-to-find ingredients in any of my recipes, which are as familiar as Lentil Soup, Turkey Wraps, and Chicken and Snow Pea Stir-Fry.

A nutritional breakdown accompanies each recipe, listing grams of carbohydrates, protein, and fat. Knowing how many grams you should consume daily will make it easy to plan meals. For example, an average woman who exercises for at least thirty minutes at least once a week should consume 109 grams of carbohydrates, 82 grams of protein, and 37 grams of fat every day. (Turn to "Eating the Right Amounts" in Chapter 1 for more detail on this.) If you follow the formula on page 269 and do a little simple math, you can devise menus that work for you.

To make this even easier, I have designed a two-week meal plan with menus that are 100 percent Zone friendly. Once you get the hang of how I put together a menu, it will become second nature for you, just as it is for me.

You will learn how to "see" if your plate is properly balanced. The protein (fish, chicken, tofu, pork) should be about the size and thickness of the palm of your hand and cover approximately a third of the plate. The rest of the plate should be filled with favorable carbohydrates and fats such as leafy greens and nonstarchy vegetables dressed with a monounsaturated oil such as olive oil. If you must eat an unfavorable carbohydrate—bread, pasta, potatoes, rice—the serving size should be no larger than a thin, tight fist.

Finally, while it's important to eat the 40-30-30 balance at every meal if at all possible, if you do not, it's easy to slip back into the Zone at your next meal. And after a while, you won't be tempted to stray. You will feel so well and happy that you won't want to lose your place in the Zone.

The human body is an amazing creation, and when it's fed right, exercised enough, and allowed to rest for at least seven consecutive hours at night, it works like a charm. And when you enter the Zone, you lead a charmed life!

Living in the Zone

I love living in the Zone, and now that it's been my life for the last decade or so, I can't imagine leaving it behind. I feel great, sleep soundly, am mentally alert, and am always ready for anything!

You will feel the same way once you make the commitment to eat and live in the Zone. I promise that life will get only better. Like me, you will walk around with a feeling of well-being and wonder how you can persuade your friends and loved ones to join you. If you are in charge of shopping and cooking in your household, you will be able to bring your family along with you into the Zone. They'll thank you. Zone-friendly meals are absolutely delicious and include the foods we all love. And there is no guilt in the Zone. If you slip up, no worries. Just resume the plan with the next meal.

I am not perfect. At some meals, I trip up or, more likely, make a conscious decision to eat foods I know are not Zone favorable. After four hours, or the next morning, I feel sluggish and unfocused. If I have eaten far too many carbohydrates, I feel worn down and have what I call a food hangover. I can't wait to get back into the Zone. And it's so easy.

Shopping in the Zone

It's important to keep a running shopping list so that when you go to the market, you are prepared. I like to shop at large natural food markets such as Whole Foods and Wild Oats markets. These stores offer the same convenient, one-stop shopping that other super-market chains do. They are not necessarily vegetarian markets; most sell wild-caught fish, free-range poultry, and responsibly raised or grass-fed beef. The produce is generally organically grown. If you don't have access to one of these markets, you can easily make wise decisions at most mainstream supermarkets.

When I go into a large market, the first place I look is the produce department. If the apples, lettuce greens, berries, and green beans don't look fresh and inviting, I walk out. If I have no choice, I buy frozen vegetables and fruit rather than fresh, which are always a good, healthful alternative. Another place to check is the fish department. If it meets my standards, my confidence meter rises! The fish should look fresh and clean, and whole fish should have bright-looking scales and gills and clear eyes. The catch should be displayed on crushed ice, and there should not be any noticeable odor. A fish department with good turnover is key.

Otherwise, I look for a well-stocked, clean store with friendly, helpful personnel. I never hesitate to ask questions and to "make friends" with the butcher, the produce manager, and the folks at the deli counter. This makes shopping more pleasant and can also save time and be of help when you're looking for something particular.

Cooking in the Zone

First and foremost, it's critical to be organized. This means know-ing what food you have on hand and what you need for the week's meals. Yes, when you live in the Zone, you have to think about food. A lot! I don't know about you, but this has never been a hardship for me.

I keep the pantry, refrigerator, and freezer stocked with Zone-friendly foods at all times. This makes it easy to prepare meals and snacks as the days go by, and so if I can't get to the market, I can stay in the Zone.

Staying in the Zone means eating three good meals a day (including breakfast) and two snacks. I eat my snacks at midafter-noon and then in the evening shortly before bed. (Turn to Chapter 2 for my two-week menu plan, to get a good idea of how to plan these meals, and see "Eating the Right Amounts" later in this chapter.) It also means never letting more than four or five hours go by without eating. If you are eating the correct Zone balance of approximately 40 percent carbohydrates to 30 percent protein and 30 percent fat based on caloric intake and using the mathematical formula on page 269, you won't feel hungry for your next meal, but you will feel ready. But don't worry. I have done the math, too, so you don't need to unless you want to.

If you have Zone-friendly food in the house or easily accessible at work, this is simple.

For this reason, when I shop, I stock up on packaged soy foods such as tofu, tempeh, soy crumbles, and soy cheeses. I buy non- or low-fat dairy cheeses, eggs, and sliced meats such as ham and turkey. If I see nice-looking smoked fish in the deli department, I buy some to snack on.

I keep containers of hummus and baba ghanouj, hard-cooked eggs, and sliced cold cuts in the refrigerator to make snacking easy. I also stock my refrigerator with olives, avocados, guacamole, and salsa, as well as lettuce greens, fresh spinach, yellow squash, zucchini, and fresh green beans. I keep a store of lemons, limes, and oranges as well as whatever other fruit or berries are in season. My favorite Zone-friendly fruits include pineapples, strawberries, blueberries, and peaches.

For nonperishable foods, I buy bags of dried beans and lentils; cans of tomatoes, cooked beans, artichoke hearts packed in brine, and low-fat chicken and vegetable broth; jars of peanut butter, almond butter, and sugar-free preserves; and packages of almonds and walnuts. I always have both regular olive oil for cooking and extra-virgin for uncooked preparations. Besides olive oil, I keep canola oil and small bottles of specialty oils such as toasted sesame, almond, and walnut.

I stock the freezer with low-glycemic frozen vegetables such as broccoli, spinach, green beans, artichoke hearts, and pea pods (not high-glycemic vegetables such as corn and English peas), frozen berries such as blueberries and strawberries, and frozen fruit such as peaches and nectarines. I also keep cooked boneless, skinless chicken breasts and shrimp in the freezer, both good sources of protein.

We are born with a hankering for sweets, but refined, processed cane sugar (white sugar) is never Zone friendly and will only create carbohydrate cravings. I satisfy my sweet tooth with whole fruit and an occasional baked good. For sweetening, I use fructose (as syrup or granules) and Splenda, a cane sugar product with rearranged molecules so that it adds sweetness without affecting insulin levels or adding calories. (Stay away from artificial sweeteners, which raise insulin levels.) After fructose and Splenda, I suggest stevia. Considered an herbal supplement, it is nearly 300 times as sweet as sugar, which makes it tricky to measure; if you use too much, the food tastes bitter. It's great for sweetening fruit and dairy products but is less successful for baked goods. Like Splenda, stevia does not affect insulin levels. My next two choices for sweetening are brown rice syrup and then honey.

I also stock up on ZonePerfect nutrition bars and ZonePerfect shakes. Both make great snacks.

Finally, I keep a few bottles of nice white and red wine in a cool storage area. A four-ounce glass is only 5 grams of carbohydrates and delightfully accentuates many meals. Depending on the brand, low-carbohydrate beers have 2 to 3 grams of carbs. I stay away from other liquor, but if you like scotch, vodka, or other spirits now and then, keep in mind that an ounce equals 9 grams of carbohydrates, so go easy.

If your tap water does not taste good, put a filter on your faucet or buy bottled water. It's important to drink eight eight-ounce glasses a day. Some liquids can be decaffeinated tea or coffee.

The Zone-Friendly Kitchen

Since cooking in the Zone does not require any special techniques or fancy equipment, most home kitchens are already there. You will need the usual equipment such as cutting boards; good, sharp knives (chef's, paring, and serrated); a good vegetable peeler; tongs;

and long-handled wooden spoons. I also suggest glass baking dishes, nonreactive mixing bowls (those not made with aluminum), a roasting pan, and good, heavy saucepans with lids. A large, non-stick skillet is extremely useful.

Without doubt, you will need an accurate kitchen scale to weigh food. Once you get in the habit of using a scale, it will become indispensable, even after you get a pretty good idea of how to guesstimate and "eyeball" most foods.

I suggest you invest in a good steamer. I like the bamboo steamers that sit in a flat pan. Equally good are stainless steel steamers fitted with a perforated inset. What I don't like are those flimsy collapsible baskets—they are nothing but frustrating.

Beyond a steamer, I suggest you outfit your kitchen with a food processor and a good, heavy-duty blender. I would be lost without either one. The blender is essential for making smoothies, and smoothies are essential for me!

A good countertop grill, as well as the grill in the backyard, makes cooking easier. Grilling is a wonderful way to cook without added fat. In wintertime, the countertop grill steps in to do the job. Finally, a slow cooker is a handy appliance, especially if you lead a hectic life. And who doesn't?

Eating Out in the Zone

If you're lucky enough to eat out, enjoy it! This is a meal that you don't have to shop for or cook. You probably are with friends or family, and the atmosphere is festive. But remember to eat in the Zone whenever possible.

This means hold the rolls, ask for extra vegetables in place of rice, pasta, or potatoes, and order a lean protein without much or any sauce. Drink water instead of alcohol, and split a dessert with a friend. If you "blow it," don't despair. Just go right back to the Zone four hours later or the next morning. I go off the Zone from time to time, but when I do, I cannot wait for my next meal to get back to the program. Because of this, I always say there is no room for guilt in the Zone!

Keeping Active in the Zone

As with any healthy lifestyle, eating right is only part of it. Exercise, stress reduction, and good sleep habits contribute to your overall well-being and, along with your food choices, are inextricably intertwined.

Everyone who can should walk for at least thirty minutes a day. This should be a brisk walk, not so strenuous that you cannot keep a conversation going but rapid enough to get your heart rate up. Divide this into three ten-minute walks if that fits more easily with your routine, but please, don't ignore it!

Beyond walking, I urge everyone to work out with weights or other resistance training (such as push-ups) two or three times a week. Ask a trainer or consult another reliable source as to what is best for your age, weight, and fitness level.

Any and all exercise fits into the Zone lifestyle: running, swimming, rowing, cross-country skiing, dancing, playing tennis, biking, working out on cardio machines at the gym—anything that gets the heart beating above its sedentary rate.

Yoga and Pilates are great for muscle toning and, when practiced regularly and correctly, are more strenuous than you might think. These disciplines also are beneficial to mental clarity.

All exercise reduces stress levels and relieves everyday aches and pains. Consult your doctor before you begin an exercise regime, but, happily, most of us can work out to some degree.

When exercise and nutritional food become part of our daily lives, stress levels go down and we tend to sleep better. This is good news, because, according to some statistics, nearly half of all Americans complain of sleep disorders at some time in their lives. I believe everyone should get at least seven hours of peaceful, uninterrupted sleep every night, although I know there are those rare individuals who exist on fewer hours. If you are sleep deprived, you have less energy, probably won't push yourself to exercise, and may eat more than you should.

If you feel tired rather than sleepy, a little exercise will help. Tie on a pair of walking shoes and hit the pavement! First, drink a glass of water; fatigue also is associated with dehydration.

Eating the Right Amounts

The Zone is devised on eating a balance of carbohydrates, protein, and fat every day. Everyone who eats a Zone-friendly diet should consume regularly scheduled daily meals and snacks that maintain a 40-30-30 balance. Sound scary? Too difficult?

It's neither scary nor difficult, as you'll discover once you get in the habit and begin cooking and eating the healthful recipes I have assembled here. You want to vary the proteins and carbohydrates you eat, and you never want to exceed the recommended amount of either. When it comes to fat, there is a little more leeway. I don't suggest filling up on sugary sweets, but a little extra olive oil won't hurt you unless you are truly trying to lose weight. Unlike carbs, fats don't affect insulin levels.

Once you get in the habit of eating in the Zone, you will be able to eyeball portion sizes and tell at a glance if you are in or out. Essentially, to be in the Zone, most of your plate should be filled with low-glycemic vegetables such as broccoli, spinach, green beans, artichoke hearts, pea pods, and other greens. Salad is always a good choice, too. Add some sliced strawberries or another fruit and you have the carbohydrates that make up 40 percent of the meal. The protein serving should be about as large and thick as the palm of your hand. Choose lean protein, such as white meat chicken, turkey, fish, and tofu. Finally, you need only a little fat to satisfy the final 30 percent. This means about a tablespoon or less of monounsaturated fat, such as olive oil or mashed avocados.

While monounsaturated fats (such as olive oil, rapeseed oil, and the fats found in almonds, peanuts, cashews, tahini, and avocados) are considered good fats, polyunsaturated fats (such as soy oil, safflower oil, and corn oil) are only fair choices and so, when you have the option, go with monounsaturated fats every time. Saturated fats (those found in animal protein and dairy products) are not healthful. Consume them sparingly, and then only in the form of lean protein and low- or nonfat dairy.

Trans fats, associated with cardiac disease, diabetes, and even some cancers, are never good for you. Trans fats are formed when hydrogen is added to vegetable oil in a process call hydrogenation, which makes the fat solid at room temperature (think of margarine) and increases the shelf life of products. Not surprisingly, the food industry has had a long-standing relationship with trans fats, which turn up in all manner of processed foods such as cookies, potato chips, candy bars, and frozen foods. As of January 1, 2006, food companies are required to begin listing trans fats on nutrition labels, where they will get their own line just below saturated fats. As well as looking for trans fats on the label, stay away from the words "partially hydrogenated," which indicate their presence as well.

Before you're comfortable eyeballing your food, you may want to understand how I get to the 40-30-30 balance. Turn to page 269 for the mathematic formula. But don't worry too much. Throughout the book, I do the heavy lifting by figuring the nutritional counts; you need only count the carbs, protein, and fat grams to put together Zone-favorable meals. Start with the Seven-Day Quick Start on page 14 and the Seven-Day Plan for Living in the Zone on page 20, and then familiarize yourself with the Food Guide on page 265 to get the idea of how to assemble meals that are squarely and deliciously in the Zone.

I have put together a general outline of how most healthy men and women should eat to stay in the Zone. It's tricky to be precise, but I think you'll get the idea. (If you are overweight, please consult with your doctor before you decide on the Zone as a weight-loss program.)

Healthy women of average weight and height who exercise moderately (thirty minutes of walking a day, for instance) should consume approximately 1,100 calories. This breaks down to:

Total each day: 109 grams of carbohydrates, 82 grams of protein, and 39 grams of fat
Each of three meals: 29 to 33 grams of carbohydrates, 22 to 24 grams of protein, and 10 to 11 grams of fat
Each of two snacks: 9 grams of carbohydrates, 7 grams of protein, and 3 grams of fat

An easy way for a healthy woman to eat right would be to consume about 3 ounces of meat or poultry, or 4½ ounces of fish at a single meal. Add a lot of fresh vegetables, a small handful of legumes, and fruit.

Healthy men of average weight and height who exercise moderately (30 minutes of walking a day, for instance) should consume approximately 1,500 calories. This breaks down to:

Total each day: 151 grams of carbohydrates, 113 grams of protein, and 50 grams of fat

Each of three meals: 43 grams of carbohydrates, 32 grams of protein, and 14 grams of fat

Each of two snacks: 11 grams of carbohydrates, 8.5 grams of protein, and 4 grams of fat

An easy way for a healthy man to eat right would be to consume about 4 ounces of meat or poultry, or 6 ounces of fish at a single meal. Add a lot of fresh vegetables, a handful of legumes, and fruit.

It's just fine for both men and women to eat a smaller breakfast than I suggest (but don't skip it altogether!) and then increase amounts proportionally throughout the day. As long as you have eaten as the day goes by and consume the appropriate amounts, all is well.

If you exercise for more than two-and-a-half hours a week and consider yourself fit, you most likely fall into the "very active" category and therefore can eat a little more at each meal. Very active women can consume 1,300 to 1,400 calories a day and very active men, 1,700 to 1,800 calories a day. For more explanation and a chart of Zone-favorable foods, turn to page 265.

Elite athletes—those who run marathons or play professional sports, for instance—have different needs. To calculate yours more precisely, go to ZonePerfect.com or call toll-free 800-390-6690.

As you get more into the Zone way of life and as your energy increases, you will probably become more active. If so, you might feel the need to increase your intake of food. The important thing is to maintain the 40-30-30 ratio and to eat regularly, without ever allowing more than four or five hours to elapse between meals.

Welcome to the Zone!

I am so happy you have decided to join me in the Zone. I have never felt better and never been more content. When winter arrives at my New England door, I don't worry as much as I once did about getting colds or the flu; I get up every morning looking forward to the day ahead; and I tackle new projects and old problems with energy and calm determination. I attribute this overall sense of gratification to the Zone.

This way of life works for most people. However, a small percentage of the population is intensely carbohydrate sensitive. Others have thyroid conditions. Menopausal women may not respond as readily to the Zone as younger women. For these folks and others whose bodies don't react easily to the 40-30-30 way of eating, I urge patience and diligence. Try the diet for a week or so, and then adjust it to meet your needs. You may have to stay away from unfavorable carbohydrates (no cheating allowed!) or increase your activity level. But stick with it. It will work, and you will feel wonderful!

Listen to your body. It will tell you how to balance your meals to keep it in the Zone. For instance, if after a week of eating a strictly Zone-friendly diet you still feel hungry for every meal and your mental sharpness is not what it should be, or you feel tired (or all three), you need more protein. If you have good mental focus but experience hunger pangs, increase your carbs. Stick with this revised diet for another week, and if you still are not perfectly balanced, try raising or reducing protein or carb levels. Like any balancing act, this one takes practice and perseverance.

The recipes on the following pages are among my favorites. All are tried and true, and many will become part of your daily Zone diet. I have attempted to keep them easy and geared to how American families eat in the early twenty-first century. Scattered throughout the pages are tips to provide encouragement along the way and help you stay in the Zone.

*T*wo-Week Menu Plan to Get You into the Zone— and Keep You There!

Being in the Zone means never having to say you're hungry. To get you started or to help you stay in the Zone, I have created a two-week menu plan. The first week jump-starts you into the Zone; the second week is representative of typical Zone menus. The food choices in the first week have very low glycemic indexes so that while you will be eating plenty and won't feel the least bit "deprived," your insulin levels will remain low. By week two, I include foods with the complex carbohydrates that raise insulin levels, although nothing in this week could be called a carb overload! In fact, this second week represents how I eat pretty much every day. I include a few breads and baked desserts, for example, but no pasta, breakfast cereal, or bready sandwiches. For even more ideas for snacks and meals, go to ZonePerfect.com and click on meal plans.

Week one will give you a jump start into the Zone, and by its end, you will feel great! Week two shows you what it will be like once you start eating in the Zone every day, week, and month of the year.

The trick to staying in the Zone is listening to your body. If you are not hungry after four hours, you ate well at your last meal. If you are hungry and also have poor mental acuity after the same period of time, you ate too many carbohydrates and not enough protein at that meal. If, on the other hand, you are ravenous but your thinking is sharp, you ate too much protein at the last meal. Try to maintain the 40-30-30 balance of carbohydrates to protein and fat; you won't get hungry and you will stay mentally alert as the day goes on.

Even if you feel like skipping a snack or a meal, don't! You can adjust quantities of food from meal to meal in any given day, as long as you eat the right amount of food during the twenty-four-hour period. Make the Zone work for you!

To enter the Zone, you must eat the dishes listed on these daily menus or substitute recipes from the book with the same ratio of fat to protein and carbohydrates. This is especially critical when you start. From breakfast through your bedtime snack, the meals I suggest are carefully crafted to help your internal system achieve the balance it needs. You will never feel hungry, you won't have cravings for sweets or fats, and you will never feel that light-headedness that comes when your blood sugar crashes because of an earlier carb overload. A word of caution: even if you are not hungry, eat everything on the daily menu, including the snacks, and drink eight glasses of water or decaffeinated coffee or tea or herbal tea.

When you eat is important, too. Never let more than four or five hours go by without refueling your body. Eat breakfast within the first hour of waking, and then eat lunch four hours later. This means, if you eat breakfast at 8 A.M., lunch will be at noon. By about 4 P.M., have an afternoon snack, which will hold you for two to three hours so that by 6:30 or 7 P.M. it will be time for dinner. Eat the bedtime snack about 9:30 or 10 P.M. so that your system will maintain its balance while you sleep. And that's all there is to it! Easy.

There are ways you may want to tailor the plan to suit your lifestyle. For example, if, because of commuting or other factors beyond your control, you find it more sensible to eat a snack at midmorning and have a late lunch, skip the afternoon snack. If you work out in the morning, eat half a ZonePerfect nutrition bar before you exercise, and then eat breakfast sixty minutes after you exercise. (The nutrition bar in this case is a "freebie.") ZonePerfect nutrition bars and shakes are easy to find in supermarkets, are easy to eat, and are perfectly balanced for the Zone way of life.

During the first week of this two-week plan, you will lose three, four, or even five pounds. This is mainly water weight, and it won't be until week two and beyond that you will lose fat, and then you will see a loss of one to two pounds a week. If you don't need to lose weight, or when you reach a plateau and want to maintain your weight, add a few more carbohydrates and be a little freer with the fats (try one or two tablespoons of olive oil rather than two teaspoons, for instance). Eat pasta in small portions and no more often than once a week. A small portion is about a third of a cup of cooked pasta. The same is true for baked desserts, such as crisps, cobblers, and cakes. Eat them only once a week and in very small portions.

To stay in the Zone, you must learn how to listen to your body and discover what works for you. You may find that you feel better sticking mainly to fruits, vegetables, and grains such as steel-cut oats and barley and staying away from wheat-based products (pasta and bread). You may decide to get your protein primarily from fish, legumes, and soy products rather than chicken and turkey. When logical, I've included leftovers. You will have to plan your meals accordingly. It's up to you how you work within the Zone. The important thing is to stay in the Zone so you will feel fully energized, alert, and ready for anything!

If your goal is to shed a few more pounds than you have after a single week, extend the Seven-Day Quick Start for a few days longer than the suggested seven. If, after just one week in the Zone, you are concerned about increasing carbohydrates and want to put it off, extend the quick start for a few more weeks. Thumb through the book and find comparable recipes. Repeat the snacks I suggest, such as sliced tomatoes with low-fat mozzarella, low-fat cottage cheese, summer cherries, and hard-cooked eggs filled with hummus. During this time, you are training your body to eat a more balanced diet. It's tough! Don't get discouraged and don't give up.

By the time you arrive at week two, the Seven-Day Plan for Living in the Zone, you will be well on your way. During this week, I introduce some foods higher on the glycemic index than most of those in week one. These include whole-grain breads and pastas and brown rice. The menus are constructed to balance these foods perfectly with others, but if you find that the increased carbohydrates are creating carb cravings, cut back on them and increase vegetables, beans, and fruits.

Seven-Day Quick Start

Day 1

Breakfast
Microwave Omelet (without optional accompaniments), page 28
Oatmeal for Five, page 40
8 ounces water, herbal or decaffeinated tea, or black decaffeinated
    coffee

Lunch
Gerdy's Vegetable Soup, page 70
4 ounces sliced turkey breast
½ cup sliced peaches
8 ounces water, herbal or decaffeinated tea, or black decaffeinated
    coffee

Afternoon Snack
½ orange
2 tablespoons low-fat cottage cheese
3 olives
1 ounce low-fat cheese
8 ounces water, herbal or decaffeinated tea, or black decaffeinated
    coffee

Dinner
Southwestern Chicken (double the recipe for leftovers), page 169
Brazilian Black Beans with Salsa, page 234
Mixed-green salad dressed with 1 tablespoon Balsamic Vinaigrette,
    page 99
½ cup cubed pineapple
8 ounces water, herbal or decaffeinated tea, or black decaffeinated
    coffee

Bedtime Snack
1 ounce roasted soybeans
8 ounces water, herbal or decaffeinated tea, or black decaffeinated
    coffee

Day 2

Breakfast
Peach-Strawberry Smoothie, page 45
8 ounces water, herbal or decaffeinated tea, or black decaffeinated
    coffee

Lunch
Gerdy's Vegetable Soup, page 70
3 ounces leftover Southwestern Chicken (Day 1 Dinner)
4 tablespoons avocado
½ cup cubed pineapple
8 ounces water, herbal or decaffeinated tea, or black decaffeinated
    coffee

Afternoon Snack
2 hard-cooked large egg whites, each filled with 1 tablespoon
    Hummus-in-the-Zone, page 65
8 ounces water, herbal or decaffeinated tea, or black decaffeinated
    coffee

Dinner
Steamed Arctic Char (double the recipe for leftovers), page 149
Kale and White Bean Salad, page 237
1 Microwave Apple, page 258
8 ounces water, herbal or decaffeinated tea, or black decaffeinated
    coffee

Bedtime Snack
1 ounce turkey breast with mustard
1 tablespoon avocado
2 slices tomato
8 ounces water, herbal or decaffeinated tea, or black decaffeinated
    coffee

Day 3

Breakfast
1 cup low-fat cottage cheese
1 cup sliced strawberries
¼ cup blueberries
¼ cup raspberries
1 peach, sliced
⅓ banana, sliced
6 teaspoons slivered almonds
8 ounces water, herbal or decaffeinated tea, or black decaffeinated
coffee

Lunch
3 ounces leftover Steamed Arctic Char (Day 2 Dinner) with Dijon-
style grainy mustard
4 tablespoons Hummus-in-the-Zone, page 65, with sliced cucumber,
carrots, and celery
½ orange
8 ounces water, herbal or decaffeinated tea, or black decaffeinated
coffee

Afternoon Snack
2 sliced tomatoes with 1 ounce low-fat mozzarella, torn fresh basil,
and sea salt
8 ounces water, herbal or decaffeinated tea, or black decaffeinated
coffee

Dinner
Chicken with Asparagus (double the recipe for leftovers), page 158
Tossed green salad dressed with 1 tablespoon Gloria's Vinaigrette,
page 98
Poached Pears, page 260
8 ounces water, herbal or decaffeinated tea, or black decaffeinated
coffee

Bedtime Snack
¾ ounce roasted or toasted soybean kernels
8 ounces water, herbal or decaffeinated tea, or black decaffeinated
coffee

Day 4

Breakfast
1 navel orange
Scrambled Eggs with Peppers, page 29
8 ounces water, herbal or decaffeinated tea, or black decaffeinated
coffee

Lunch
3 ounces leftover Chicken with Asparagus (Day 3 Dinner)
1 apple
3 almonds
8 ounces water, herbal or decaffeinated tea, or black decaffeinated
coffee

Afternoon Snack
½ ZonePerfect shake
8 ounces water, herbal or decaffeinated tea, or black decaffeinated
coffee

Dinner
Haddock with Artichoke Hearts, page 140
Lentil Soup, page 67
Jicama Slaw, page 96
½ cup sliced strawberries
8 ounces water, herbal or decaffeinated tea, or black decaffeinated
coffee

Bedtime Snack
½ cup plain yogurt with 1 teaspoon pure vanilla extract
1½ teaspoons slivered almonds
8 ounces water, herbal or decaffeinated tea, or black decaffeinated
coffee

Day 5

Breakfast
Zone Fruit Pudding (make enough for leftovers), page 41
8 ounces water, herbal or decaffeinated tea, or black decaffeinated
coffee

Lunch
Lentil Soup, page 67
3½ ounces tuna with lemon juice
4 tablespoons avocado
1 slice tomato with 2 olives and lettuce
8 ounces water, herbal or decaffeinated tea, or black decaffeinated coffee

Afternoon Snack
2 hard-cooked large egg whites, each filled with 1 tablespoon store-bought baba ghanouj
8 ounces water, herbal or decaffeinated tea, or black decaffeinated coffee

Dinner
Sautéed Turkey Breast with Mushrooms and Garlic, page 192
White Beans with Spinach and Shirataki (make enough for leftovers), page 232
Tangy Coleslaw, page 97
⅓ cup The Best Applesauce, page 259
8 ounces water, herbal or decaffeinated tea, or black decaffeinated coffee

Bedtime Snack
4 ounces wine
1 ounce low-fat cheese
3 almonds
8 ounces water, herbal or decaffeinated tea, or black decaffeinated coffee

Day 6

Breakfast
3 ounces Zone Fruit Pudding (Day 5 Breakfast)
8 ounces water, herbal or decaffeinated tea, or black decaffeinated coffee

Lunch
Turkey-Apple Quesadilla, page 193
3 ounces White Beans with Spinach and Shirataki (Day 5 Dinner)

8 ounces water, herbal or decaffeinated tea, or black decaffeinated coffee

Afternoon Snack
½ ZonePerfect nutrition bar
8 ounces water, herbal or decaffeinated tea, or black decaffeinated coffee

Dinner
Scallops with Orange and Sesame Oil, page 115
Wilted Garlic Spinach, page 240
1 Chocolate-Covered Strawberry, page 263
8 ounces water, herbal or decaffeinated tea, or black decaffeinated coffee

Bedtime Snack
¾ cup low-fat milk or soy milk
3 almonds
8 ounces water, herbal or decaffeinated tea, or black decaffeinated coffee

Day 7

Breakfast
Oatmeal for Five (with 1 scoop protein powder), page 40
3 (1-ounce) soy sausages or 3 ounces lean Canadian bacon
8 ounces water, herbal or decaffeinated tea, or black decaffeinated coffee

Lunch
Salad bar, page 77
8 ounces water, herbal or decaffeinated tea, or black decaffeinated coffee

Afternoon Snack
2 hard-cooked egg whites, each stuffed with 1 tablespoon Hummus-in-the-Zone, page 65
8 ounces water, herbal or decaffeinated tea, or black decaffeinated coffee

Dinner
Poached Snapper alla Livornese, page 130
12 spears steamed asparagus
Apple Crisp, page 257
8 ounces water, herbal or decaffeinated tea, or black decaffeinated
  coffee

Bedtime Snack
4 ounces white or red wine
1 ounce low-fat cheese or cooked chicken
6 peanuts
8 ounces water, herbal or decaffeinated tea, or black decaffeinated
  coffee

Seven-Day Plan for Living in the Zone

Day 1

Breakfast
Blueberry Smoothie, page 44
8 ounces water, herbal or decaffeinated tea, or black decaffeinated
  coffee

Lunch
2 frozen, packaged soy burgers with lettuce and your favorite salsa
1 Microwave Apple, page 258
8 ounces water, herbal or decaffeinated tea, or black decaffeinated
  coffee

Afternoon Snack
½ ZonePerfect nutrition bar
8 ounces water, herbal or decaffeinated tea, or black decaffeinated
  coffee

Dinner
Salmon with Orange and Miso Sauce (double the recipe for
  leftovers), page 121
String Beans with Sesame Seeds, page 224

Mixed-green salad dressed with 1 tablespoon lemon juice
Sweet Crisps with Ricotta and Berries, page 255
8 ounces water, herbal or decaffeinated tea, or black decaffeinated
coffee

Bedtime Snack
½ cup plain yogurt with 1 teaspoon pure vanilla extract
1½ teaspoons slivered almonds
8 ounces water, herbal or decaffeinated tea, or black decaffeinated
coffee

Day 2

Breakfast
Spanish Scrambled Eggs, page 32
½ nectarine or peach
8 ounces water, herbal or decaffeinated tea, or black decaffeinated
coffee

Lunch
3 ounces leftover Salmon with Orange and Miso Sauce (Day 1 Dinner)
8 ounces water, herbal or decaffeinated tea, or black decaffeinated
coffee

Afternoon Snack
½ cup cooked edamame
8 ounces water, herbal or decaffeinated tea, or black decaffeinated
coffee

Dinner
Grilled Chicken and Fennel with Spicy Orange Glaze, page 175
Tossed green salad dressed with 1 tablespoon Gloria's Vinaigrette,
page 98
¼ cup The Best Applesauce, page 259
8 ounces water, herbal or decaffeinated tea, or black decaffeinated
coffee

Bedtime Snack
¼ cup low-fat cottage cheese

¼ cup The Best Applesauce, page 259

3 almonds

8 ounces water, herbal or decaffeinated tea, or black decaffeinated
coffee

Day 3

Breakfast
Apple Crisp, page 257

1 cup low-fat cottage cheese

8 ounces water, herbal or decaffeinated tea, or black decaffeinated
coffee

Lunch
12 ounces Marinated Nigari Tofu, page 207, or packaged grilled tofu,
or 4 ounces cooked chicken

1½ cups frozen Chinese (or other) vegetables with ¼ cup kidney
beans

½ cup cubed pineapple

8 ounces water, herbal or decaffeinated tea, or black decaffeinated
coffee

Afternoon Snack
½ Microwave Apple, page 258

1 ounce low-fat cheddar cheese or soy cheese

1 macadamia nut

8 ounces water, herbal or decaffeinated tea, or black decaffeinated
coffee

Dinner
1 Asian Turkey Burger, page 197

Grilled Eggplant with Hoisin Sauce, page 229

Tangy Coleslaw, page 97

1 Chocolate-Covered Strawberry, page 263

8 ounces water, herbal or decaffeinated tea, or black decaffeinated
coffee

Bedtime Snack
4 ounces wine

1½ ounces cooked shrimp
3 olives
8 ounces water, herbal or decaffeinated tea, or black decaffeinated coffee

Day 4

Breakfast
Sunday Brunch Bagels with Smoked Fish, page 37
8 ounces water, herbal or decaffeinated tea, or black decaffeinated coffee

Lunch
Tempeh-Vegetable Salad, page 212
2 rye crisp crackers
1 cup sliced jicama
½ to 1 cucumber, sliced
½ cup white or red seedless grapes
8 ounces water, herbal or decaffeinated tea, or black decaffeinated coffee

Afternoon Snack
8 ounces soy milk or skim milk
6 peanuts
8 ounces water, herbal or decaffeinated tea, or black decaffeinated coffee

Dinner
Grilled Lemon-Basil Pork Chop, page 202
Mesclun Greens with Roasted Red Peppers, Portobello Mushrooms, and Feta, page 83
1 Chocolate-Covered Strawberry, page 263
8 ounces water, herbal or decaffeinated tea, or black decaffeinated coffee

Bedtime Snack
½ ZonePerfect nutrition bar
8 ounces water, herbal or decaffeinated tea, or black decaffeinated coffee

Day 5

Breakfast
Zone Fruit Pudding, page 41
8 ounces water, herbal or decaffeinated tea, or black decaffeinated
   coffee

Lunch
Open-Face Avocado-Chicken Salad Sandwich, page 184
8 ounces water, herbal or decaffeinated tea, or black decaffeinated
   coffee

Afternoon Snack
3 slices tofurkey or 1 ounce cooked turkey with mustard
8 ounces water, herbal or decaffeinated tea, or black decaffeinated
   coffee

Dinner
Roasted Teriyaki Turkey Breast, page 190
Mixed-green salad dressed with 1 tablespoon Balsamic Vinaigrette,
   page 99
Steamed Summer Squash, page 225
Summer Fruit Crisp, page 254
8 ounces water, herbal or decaffeinated tea, or black decaffeinated
   coffee

Bedtime Snack
1 ounce low-fat cheese
4 ounces white or red wine
8 ounces water, herbal or decaffeinated tea, or black decaffeinated
   coffee

Day 6

Breakfast
Microwave Omelet, page 28
8 ounces water, herbal or decaffeinated tea, or black decaffeinated
   coffee

Lunch

Tuna and Apple Salad, page 79

8 ounces water, herbal or decaffeinated tea, or black decaffeinated
coffee

Afternoon Snack

1 ounce roasted soybeans

8 ounces water, herbal or decaffeinated tea, or black decaffeinated
coffee

Dinner

Chicken Cacciatore, page 171

Whipped Cauliflower, page 241

Israeli Chopped Salad, page 95

½ cup sliced strawberries

8 ounces water, herbal or decaffeinated tea, or black decaffeinated
coffee

Bedtime Snack

¼ cup Summer Fruit Crisp, page 254

¼ cup low-fat cottage cheese

8 ounces water, herbal or decaffeinated tea, or black decaffeinated
coffee

Day 7

Breakfast

Baked Eggs with Zucchini and Tomatoes, page 34

1 grapefruit

1 slice high-fiber bread

1 teaspoon peanut butter

8 ounces water, herbal or decaffeinated tea, or black decaffeinated
coffee

Lunch

Kale and White Bean Salad, page 237

1 serving leftover Chicken Cacciatore (Day 6 Dinner)

8 ounces water, herbal or decaffeinated tea, or black decaffeinated
coffee

Afternoon Snack
⅓ cup cooked edamame
8 ounces water, herbal or decaffeinated tea, or black decaffeinated
coffee

Dinner
Hoisin-Wasabi Sablefish, page 142
Chick-Peas with Broccoli Rabe, page 245
Cucumber Salad, page 76
1 Chocolate-Covered Strawberry, page 263
8 ounces water, herbal or decaffeinated tea, or black decaffeinated
coffee

Bedtime Snack
½ Microwave Apple, page 258
1 ounce soy cheese or low-fat cheddar cheese
3 almonds
8 ounces water, herbal or decaffeinated tea, or black decaffeinated
coffee

What I hope you take away from this two-week plan is how to eat balanced meals and about how much food you need to stay in the Zone. This should help you assemble your own menus using my recipes or, perhaps, rely on some favorites from your personal recipe file. The trick is to maintain the 40–30–30 ratio of carbohydrates to protein and fat.

Over the course of the two weeks, I frequently tell you to double a recipe or make enough of a particular dish for another meal. My husband and I love my recipe for Oatmeal for Five on page 40. So during the cold New England winters, I make a big pot and then portion it into half-pound containers. These keep in the refrigerator for a few weeks and are easy to heat in the microwave. This is only one suggestion, but you get the idea. Think about ways to work Zone-friendly foods into your daily life so that it's never a chore but always a pleasure to eat in the Zone.

Breakfast

Microwave Omelet

I include this omelet in the breakfast chapter, but it's equally good for lunch when you want something quick and healthful. When I worked in an office, I took egg substitute and the rest of the fixin's in with me and made this in the office microwave. It's that easy!

Serves 1

6 white or cremini mushrooms, sliced
¼ cup chopped yellow onion
Olive oil cooking spray
¾ cup egg substitute, or 3 whole eggs or 5 egg whites, lightly
    beaten
2 slices (1 ounce) soy cheese or low-fat cheese, such as Monterey
    Jack or cheddar, halved
About 6 drops of hot red pepper sauce
Herbamare
Freshly ground pepper
1 slice rye or whole-grain bread, optional
2 teaspoons almond butter or peanut butter, optional
¼ cup Salsa-in-the-Zone, page 235, optional
½ cup sliced strawberries, optional
½ grapefruit, optional

1. In a microwave-safe bowl, mix together the mushrooms and onion, and microwave at High for 1 minute, or until the vegetables soften. Drain and discard any liquid that collects in the bowl.

2. Spray a shallow, wide, microwave-safe bowl with olive oil cooking spray. Pour the egg substitute into the bowl. Microwave at High for 2 minutes. Remove the bowl from the microwave, add the cheese, and stir gently with a fork. Microwave at High for 1 minute and 30 seconds longer, or until the eggs are partially set. Stir again, add the

reserved vegetables, and stir gently to mix. Microwave at High for 1 minute longer, or until the eggs are set. Season with hot sauce, Herbamare, and pepper to taste.

3. Meanwhile, if choosing, toast the bread and spread it with nut butter. Serve the omelet with the salsa, fruit, and toast on the side.

Per serving: 4 grams carbohydrates, 28 grams protein, 3 grams fat

Scrambled Eggs with Peppers

When you complement these scrambled eggs with a dish of fresh fruit, your carbohydrate intake for the morning will be complete. I suggest orange or nectarine slices and fresh strawberries, but you choose your favorites. As are most other recipes for scrambled eggs, this one is forgiving: If you don't like chili peppers, leave that ingredient out. It provides nothing more than flavor. If you would rather substitute zucchini or asparagus for the bell peppers, go right ahead. It's all about personal taste.

Serves 1

2 teaspoons olive oil
½ large yellow onion, diced
1½ green, red, or yellow bell peppers, thinly diced
1 garlic clove, minced
¼ small fresh chili or jalapeño pepper, seeded and finely chopped
1 whole egg
¾ cup egg whites (about 6)
Sea salt and freshly ground pepper, or Herbamare
2 medium tomatoes, chopped

1. In a nonstick skillet, heat 1 teaspoon of the olive oil over medium heat. Add the onion and cook, stirring, for about 5 minutes, until it begins to soften. Add the bell peppers, garlic, and chili, and stir to mix. Cover and cook over low heat for 10 minutes, or until the vegetables are softened. Transfer the vegetables to a bowl.

2. Meanwhile, whisk together the egg, egg whites, and salt and pepper to taste.

3. In the same skillet, heat the remaining teaspoon of oil over low heat. Pour the eggs into the pan and cook, stirring gently with a wooden spoon, for about 3 minutes, until the eggs are softly scrambled. Stir and scrape all around the bottom of the pan as the eggs scramble. Do not overcook; the eggs should be creamy rather than set.

4. Stir the tomatoes into the peppers. Spoon the vegetables over the eggs, adjust the seasonings, and serve immediately.

Per serving: 13 grams carbohydrates, 24 grams protein, 9 grams fat

Zone Tip
Try to spend 20 minutes outside every day to get your minimum vitamin D supply. If you live in a cold climate, take 400 IU of vitamin D from November through March. It makes up for the lack of sunshine.

Mushroom and Goat Cheese Omelet

Omelets turn ordinary eggs into something special, and this one is no exception. The mushrooms, goat cheese, and sun-dried tomatoes work together to create a wonderfully rich breakfast that could very well be eaten for weekend brunch or for supper. To round out your carbohydrate allowance, serve this with a bowl of oatmeal, a sliced apple, or a cup of sliced strawberries. Use your favorite kind of goat cheese, but if you are not loyal to one particular brand, read the labels and go for the one with the lowest fat—and no more than 6 grams per serving.

When I cook this omelet, I begin with a nonstick pan and let it get hot before I add the oil. When the oil slides easily over the pan's surface, it's time to pour in the eggs. This small step helps prevent sticking even though you are using a modest amount of oil.

Serves 1

¼ cup sun-dried tomatoes
Olive oil cooking spray
1 shallot, minced
1 garlic clove, minced
1 large fresh or dried portobello mushroom, diced*
¼ cup thinly sliced basil leaves
½ teaspoon sea salt
¼ teaspoon pepper
1 cup egg substitute or egg whites
2 tablespoons low-fat milk or soy milk
1 teaspoon olive oil
1 ounce goat cheese

1. In a small bowl, soak the tomatoes in hot tap water for about 20 minutes, until softened. Drain and chop coarsely.

2. Spray a small skillet with olive oil cooking spray and set it over medium heat. When the skillet is hot, sauté the shallot and garlic for about 1 minute, until they are translucent. Add the mushroom and cook for about 2 minutes, stirring, until softened. Stir in the sun-dried tomatoes, half of the basil, and half of the salt and pepper. Transfer the contents to a bowl and set it aside.

3. In a mixing bowl, whisk the eggs and milk with the remaining salt and pepper.

4. Heat a large skillet over high heat. Add the olive oil, and when it is hot enough to slide evenly over the surface to coat it, pour the eggs into the pan. As the eggs cook, use a heat-resistant rubber spatula to lift the edges so that the liquid portions run underneath. This will help the eggs set better. After about 1 minute and when the eggs begin to set and brown lightly on the bottom, carefully turn the omelet over.

5. Spread the mushroom filling onto half of the omelet, and sprinkle the goat cheese on top. Cook about 3 to 4 minutes longer. Slide the omelet onto a plate, folding it over on itself as you do. Sprinkle with the remaining basil for garnish.

Per serving: 16 grams carbohydrates, 25 grams protein, 12 grams fat

*If you're using a dried portobello mushroom, soak it in hot tap water for about 20 minutes, until softened. Drain and chop.

> **Zone Tip**
> Caffeine and artificially sweetened sodas may raise your insulin level and take you out of the Zone. I avoid them.

Spanish Scrambled Eggs

For a complete Zone-friendly meal, try this Spanish omelet, and feel free to substitute another vegetable for the string beans or asparagus. You might prefer bell peppers, broccoli, or summer squash. Steam the vegetables lightly before sautéing them, and when you cook the eggs, stir them only enough to mix. Your goal is an omelet that is more vegetable than egg, and one in which the egg whites are more obvious than the yellow yolk.

I developed this recipe after spending time visiting my daughter when she studied in Seville, Spain, a few years ago. I was impressed with the food at the local restaurants in that sunny country—fresh and light and served in reasonable-sized portions, and the only fat in sight was truly delicious, fruity olive oil! We particularly liked eating in tapas bars, where, for very little money, we could sample small bites of a wide range of dishes, enjoyed with a glass of robust Spanish wine or beer. The tapas were extremely Zone friendly, I found. They were made with shrimp, squid, free-range chicken, juicy tomatoes, bell peppers, slender asparagus, onions, string beans, potatoes, and very often eggs, which translated into high-protein meals made with olive oil, perfect for the traveler wishing to stay in the Zone with a 40-30-30 balance of carbohydrates to protein and fat.

Serves 1

½ cup peeled and cubed potato
5 ounces string beans, cut into bite-size pieces (about 1 cup)
8 ounces asparagus, cut into bite-size pieces (about 1 cup)
2 teaspoons olive oil
½ cup egg whites (3 to 4)
1 whole egg
Sea salt and freshly ground pepper
Herbamare

1. In a steaming basket set over boiling water, steam the potato, beans, and asparagus for 5 minutes, or until the vegetables begin to soften.

2. In a nonstick sauté pan, heat the olive oil over medium heat. Add the steamed vegetables and sauté for about 3 minutes, until the vegetables are tender and cooked through.

3. Reduce the heat to medium-low and add the egg whites. Cook for about 30 seconds, until they begin to set and turn white. Crack the egg into the pan, as you would for a sunny-side up egg, and cook for about 30 seconds, until the white sets.

4. Using a nonmetal fork or spoon, slowly start stirring the eggs as they cook. Cook for about 3 minutes, until the eggs are done the way you like them. Season to taste with the salt, pepper, and Herbamare. Serve immediately.

Per serving: 23 grams carbohydrates, 20 grams protein, 5 grams fat

---

Zone Tip

Set small goals each week, regardless of how long you have been in the Zone. For instance, if you like caffeinated coffee, try to decrease caffeine gradually by replacing it with decaffeinated coffee until you are drinking only decaf! Small goals are easier to attain.

Baked Eggs with Zucchini and Tomatoes

I love this baked breakfast dish—it's so civilized to begin the day by sitting down to a table set with place mats, napkins, and a bubbling egg casserole filled with leeks, zucchini, and mushrooms and topped with sliced tomatoes and melted cheese. I use soy cheese for this, but if you want to substitute dairy cheese, be sure to use low-fat cheeses. To make this a complete Zone meal, include fresh seasonal fruit and a slice of rye toast with each serving.

Serves 4

2 teaspoons olive oil
1 leek, white part only, thinly sliced
3 small zucchini (about 6 inches long), or 2 larger zucchini, diced
½ cup quartered white mushrooms
Herbamare
Sea salt and freshly ground pepper
4 whole eggs
1½ cups egg whites (about 10)
2 tablespoons veggie (soy) cream cheese
Olive oil cooking spray
¼ cup grated soy Parmesan cheese
¼ cup shredded soy mozzarella cheese
2 tomatoes sliced, with the slices cut into half-moons
1 tablespoon chopped fresh basil

1. Preheat the oven to 350°F.

2. In a nonstick skillet, heat the olive oil over medium-high heat. When the oil is hot, cook the leek for 2 to 3 minutes, or until it begins to soften. Add the zucchini and mushrooms and sauté for 5 minutes. Season to taste with Herbamare, salt, and pepper. Transfer to a colander set over a bowl to drain off any liquid.

3. In a food processor fitted with the metal blade or in a blender, process the eggs, egg whites, and cream cheese until smooth. Again, season to taste with Herbamare, salt, and pepper, and pulse to mix.

4. Spray a 2-quart casserole dish with olive oil cooking spray. Pour in the egg mixture and top with the drained vegetables. Scatter the Parmesan and mozzarella cheeses over the top and bake for 30 minutes, or until the eggs are firm. When the eggs are set, pull the casserole from the oven, lay the tomato slices over the top, and sprinkle with basil. Return the casserole to the oven and bake for about 10 minutes longer, until the tomatoes soften, the cheese

browns lightly, and the casserole is hot all the way through and firm to the touch.

Per serving: 6 grams carbohydrates, 28 grams protein, 3.5 grams fat

Tofu Scramble

I eat a lot of tofu, partly because it's such a good source of protein and also because it's so versatile. It literally assumes the flavor of the seasonings you add to it. In this simple breakfast scramble, the tofu grabs the flavor of the Herbamare, which is one of my favorite seasonings and is found in health food stores. It contains sea salt that has been seeped in a variety of herbs. To get enough protein from tofu, remember that 3 ounces equals about 7 grams of protein. Try this with a cup of oatmeal: the scramble for protein, the oatmeal for carbohydrates.

Serves 1

9 ounces firm or extra-firm tofu
1 teaspoon olive oil
Herbamare
Pinch of ground cinnamon

1. Lift the block of tofu from the package and gently press it between your fingers to remove any excess water. Wrap the tofu in a double thickness of cheesecloth or a clean kitchen towel, set it on a plate, and set another plate on top of it. Place heavy cans or other weights on the top plate to compress the tofu for 15 minutes.

2. Unwrap the tofu and cut it into small cubes, about 1 inch square.

3. In a nonstick skillet set over medium heat, heat the olive oil. Add the tofu and stir-fry for about 1 minute. Season to taste with Herbamare and cinnamon, and stir-fry for about 10 minutes longer, until golden brown.

Per serving: 0 grams carbohydrates, 21 grams protein, 9 grams fat

---

Zone Tip

If you are new to the Zone, try establishing small routines. Find a breakfast that works for you and make sure you eat it within the first hour of waking. Go slowly for the best success. All changes must be made in baby steps before they can become a permanent part of your life.

Sunday Brunch Bagels with Smoked Fish

This is one of my favorite morning indulgences, and because it fills me up, I am able to go for 5 hours before I need to eat lunch or have a snack. Start with a whole-grain bagel and get right into the breaded center with your fingers to pull as much of it from the bagel crust as you can. If you crave carbohydrates or feel a little sluggish a few hours after you eat this, you may be insulin sensitive, in which case, up the fat by about 3 grams, perhaps by adding 3 almonds. If you know you are insulin sensitive, eat only ¼ of the bagel and also eat ½ grapefruit with the meal. Veggie cream cheese is made from soy and is sold alongside the other soy products in most supermarkets.

Serves 1

½ whole-grain plain bagel
2 tablespoons veggie (soy) cream cheese
1 small cucumber (about 2 inches long), sliced into rounds
1 thin slice sweet onion, such as Vidalia, Walla Walla, or Maui
4 ounces smoked salmon or another kind of smoked fish, such as
     sturgeon or sablefish
3 thin slices tomato

1. Using your fingers, pull the breading from the bagel half to leave
a shell with just a thin layer of bread. Discard the breading or reserve
it for bread crumbs.

2. Spread the cream cheese in the bagel shell. Top with the
cucumber and onion slices and then with the smoked fish and tomato
slices.

Per serving: 28 grams carbohydrates, 25 grams protein, 9 grams fat

---

Zone Tip

The glycemic index is a measurement of how quickly
carbohydrates are metabolized into glucose and consequently
into your blood sugar. The index is based on white bread being at
100. Always try to use foods with a mid- to low-glycemic index in
order to have a tight control of blood sugar levels. Most fruits
and vegetables have mid- to low-glycemic levels, while baked
goods have high levels.

Turkey Wrap

Turkey for breakfast? Why not! I like to mix it with grapes and some
soft, mashed avocado, which moistens it much the same way mayon-

naise does but with a healthful fat and loads of great flavor. This is a terrific breakfast anytime, but especially if you are running late and need to eat in the car or while walking to the train.

Serves 1

3 ounces turkey, torn or shredded
1 cup halved white or red seedless grapes
2 tablespoons mashed avocado (about ⅓ avocado)
Herbamare
Freshly ground pepper
1 6-inch wheat tortilla

1. In a mixing bowl, toss together the turkey and grapes. Add the avocado and stir until well mixed. Season to taste with the Herbamare and pepper.

2. Warm the tortilla in a dry pan, on a countertop grill, in a toaster oven, or under the broiler for about 30 seconds on each side.

3. Spoon the turkey mixture down the center of the tortilla. Fold it around the filling and serve.

Per serving: 35 grams carbohydrates, 22 grams protein, 9 grams fat

Zone Tip
If you are having trouble with meal ideas for breakfast and are sick of eggs, try an unconventional breakfast of leftovers from lunch or dinner. It's all good!

Oatmeal for Five

If I had to name my all-time comfort food, it would be oatmeal. When I was a child, my grandfather topped it with a little cinnamon and sugar, a pat of butter, and the cream poured off the top of the milk bottle, and I loved it! It was the only thing he made, otherwise deferring to my grandmother in all kitchen matters, but I developed a fondness for it. Much later, when I found myself living through long, cold Boston winters, I started making my own version with raisins, cinnamon, and apples. This became our standard family breakfast (we even ate it on Christmas morning!), but when I started eating in the Zone, I omitted the raisins. I love the recipe here and eat it just about daily, although during the summer months I use fresh berries exclusively and might plop in some sliced fresh peaches and nectarines. The almond butter is optional. For instance, if you eat a protein-rich food with fat alongside the oatmeal, forget the almond butter.

Serves 5

1 cup steel-cut oats
1 apple, peeled and chopped
¼ teaspoon ground cinnamon
15 fresh or frozen strawberries, hulled and quartered
About 50 fresh or frozen raspberries
About 50 fresh or frozen blueberries
5 tablespoons creamy almond butter or peanut butter, or 1 cup slivered almonds, optional
1⅔ cups soy milk or skim milk

1. In a saucepan, bring a quart of water to a boil over medium-high heat. Add the oats, apple, and cinnamon, and return to a boil. Reduce the heat to low, and cook gently for 35 to 40 minutes, stirring occasionally, until the oatmeal is thick and cooked through.

2. If serving right away, add the berries, raise the heat, and cook for about 2 minutes, stirring gently. If serving later, add the berries just before serving when you reheat the oatmeal.

3. Garnish with almond butter and soy milk.

Per serving: 29 grams carbohydrates, 2 grams protein, 9 grams fat

---

Zone Tip

In order to get your metabolism going, eat within an hour of waking. If you do not have a big appetite in the morning or if you work out first thing, eat half of a ZonePerfect nutrition bar, and then 30 to 60 minutes later, have breakfast.

Zone Fruit Pudding

This is great to have in the refrigerator for easy breakfasts and quick snacks. A food processor or blender turns the cottage cheese and yogurt into a smooth, satisfying mixture that contrasts with the fruit and nuts, and the Splenda adds just enough sweetness. As discussed in Chapter 1, Splenda is a natural sweetener made from cane sugar with rearranged molecules so that it is calorie free and does not raise insulin production.

Serves 2

1 cup low-fat plain yogurt
1 cup low-fat cottage cheese
1 teaspoon nonalcoholic vanilla flavoring*
2 tablespoons Splenda
1 cup sliced strawberries
½ cup blueberries

1 peach, peeled and sliced
⅓ banana, sliced
15 toasted almonds, coarsely chopped (about ¼ cup)* (See note on
    page 92 for toasting pecans.)

1. In a food processor fitted with the metal blade or in a blender, combine the yogurt, cottage cheese, vanilla, and Splenda, and process until smooth.

2. In another bowl, gently mix the strawberries, blueberries, peach, and banana.

3. Scatter half of the almonds in the bottom of a glass pie plate and then top with the fruit. Spoon the pureed yogurt mixture over the fruit. Sprinkle the remaining nuts on top. Cover with plastic wrap and refrigerate for at least 1 hour and up to 8 hours.

Per serving: 30 grams carbohydrates, 23 grams protein, 7.5 grams fat

*You can substitute 1 teaspoon nonalcoholic banana or strawberry flavoring for the vanilla. If you choose to use fat-free cottage cheese and fat-free yogurt, increase the number of almonds to 30.

Tofu Shake-Pudding

For an easy breakfast, nothing beats this. Make it the night before and refrigerate it so that it's ready when you are. For the best texture and the most protein, be sure to use firm or extra-firm silken tofu.

Serves 1

½ cup soy milk

9 ounces firm or extra-firm silken tofu*

2 tablespoons (½ scoop) protein powder*

1 cup fresh or frozen strawberries or fresh or frozen raspberries

⅓ banana

3 tablespoons chopped almonds, or 1 tablespoon almond butter

1 tablespoon Splenda

½ teaspoon nonalcoholic banana or strawberry flavoring

1. Put the soy milk in a blender and add the tofu, protein powder, strawberries, banana, almonds, Splenda, and flavoring. Blend until smooth. You may have to turn off the blender and stir the ingredients once or twice with a spoon and blend again to reach the desired consistency.

2. Refrigerate for at least 1 hour and up to 8 hours before serving cold.

Per serving: 36 grams carbohydrates, 28 grams protein, 12 grams fat

*Extra-firm silken tofu is not easy to find. Mori-Nu makes it and sells it in 12-ounce aseptic packages that do not need refrigeration until opened. If you cannot find it, use any kind of tofu you like, but the texture of the shake will not be as smooth, and the protein count will be a little lower.

Protein powder is sold at health food stores and many supermarkets. Look for a brand with at least 14 grams of protein per serving or scoop.

Zone Tip

Good sources of isolated protein powders include egg and milk combinations and lactose-free whey powder. For vegetarians, isolated soy protein powders are an excellent choice. In both cases, the powders can be added to carbohydrate-rich foods to make them more balanced.

Blueberry Smoothie

If you like blueberries, you will adore this smoothie. It just tastes like summertime! When blueberries are in season and the price is low, I buy five or six pints and freeze most of them in a zipped plastic freezer bag. For the right texture, you should use extra-silken tofu or just extra-firm tofu. Both come in vacuum-sealed packages with long shelf lives. I buy several and keep them on hand so that I can make smoothies anytime. While the packages don't require refrigeration until they are opened, I store them in the refrigerator so that they are nice and cold.

Serves 1

1 cup chilled soy milk or skim milk
1½ cups fresh or frozen blueberries
9 ounces firm or extra-firm silken tofu
1½ tablespoons chopped walnuts
1 tablespoon Splenda
1 teaspoon nonalcoholic banana or vanilla flavoring

1. Combine all ingredients in a blender and blend on high speed until smooth. Drink immediately.

Per serving: 36 grams carbohydrates, 23 grams protein, 12 grams fat

Zone Tip

The first two weeks in the Zone are the most difficult for your body. Your body is adjusting to getting its energy from carbohydrates instead of from fat. If your body craves an unfavorable carbohydrate or extra carbohydrates, have them in the evening. Breakfast and lunch are too important, and you eat these meals at the times of day when you most need your energy and mental sharpness.

Peach-Strawberry Smoothie

Where I live in Boston, we call thick milkshakes "frappés." Believe me, I could name this a Peach-Strawberry Frappé and be accurate! It's that thick and delicious. If you don't eat much tofu, this is a good way to begin, and if you don't have flaxseed oil, substitute a little walnut oil.

Serves 1

1 cup chilled soy milk or skim milk
1 cup sliced fresh or frozen peaches
9 ounces firm or extra-firm silken tofu (see note on page 43)
1 cup fresh or frozen strawberries
4 whole almonds
1 tablespoon Splenda
2 teaspoons flaxseed oil
1 teaspoon nonalcoholic strawberry flavoring

1. Combine all ingredients in a blender and blend on high speed until smooth. Drink immediately.

Per serving: 36 grams carbohydrates, 23 grams protein, 16 grams fat

$\mathcal{A}$ppetizers, Soups, and Salads

Crunchy Soy and Peanut Appetizers

Serving tasty, easy fillings in lettuce leaves for appetizers is a good way to get around the more traditional custom of serving bread or crackers topped with spreads. This filling is made with soy crumbles, which are easy to find and provide good body and texture alongside the crunchy peanuts and slaw. This recipe is easily doubled or tripled for larger gatherings.

Serves 6

Olive oil cooking spray
⅔ cup ground soy crumbles
⅔ cup packaged coleslaw
2 tablespoons chopped unsalted peanuts
2 tablespoons hoisin sauce
Hot sauce
6 large leaves Boston or Bibb lettuce

1. In a small nonstick skillet lightly coated with olive oil spray, sauté the soy crumbles, stirring, for about 5 minutes, until browned.

2. Transfer the soy crumbles to a bowl and add the coleslaw, peanuts, hoisin sauce, and hot sauce to taste.

3. Fill each lettuce leaf with a spoonful of the soy mixture. Serve soon after preparing, so that they don't become soggy.

Per serving: 3 grams carbohydrates, 4 grams protein, 2 grams fat

> **Zone Tip**
> Eating in the Zone deters overeating. Because you must eat a
> meal every 4 or 5 hours, and have two snacks as well, you never
> feel famished. It's that famished feeling that brings on cravings.
> This results in overeating and means that your body cannot
> process food efficiently, and so it stores the excess as fat.

Artichoke Torte

A warm, creamy artichoke torte topped with stringy melted cheese
is a great appetizer or snack. Eat it alone or spooned on top of
celery sticks or whole wheat pita wedges. I like to keep frozen artichoke hearts on hand for this recipe and many others in the book.
They make cooking so easy, and their nutty, slightly acidic flavor
adds a lot to so many dishes. Clearly, they are one of my favorites!

Serves 6

Olive oil cooking spray
2 9-ounce packages frozen artichoke hearts
¼ cup plus 1 tablespoon fresh whole wheat bread crumbs
2 teaspoons olive oil
½ cup chopped scallion, white and green parts
½ teaspoon dried oregano
2 tablespoons chopped flat-leaf parsley
¾ cup egg substitute or egg whites
¾ cup grated soy Parmesan cheese
¾ cup low-fat milk or soy milk
Sea salt and freshly ground pepper

1. Preheat the oven to 375°F. Coat an 8-inch square baking pan with olive oil cooking spray.

2. Cook the artichokes according to package directions. Drain and chop into bite-size pieces.

3. Sprinkle the 1 tablespoon bread crumbs in the bottom of the pan, and spread the artichokes on top.

4. In a medium skillet, heat the olive oil over medium heat and sauté the scallion, oregano, and parsley for 2 to 3 minutes, until the scallion starts to soften. Remove from the heat.

5. In a mixing bowl, stir together the egg substitute, Parmesan, milk, and remaining ¼ cup bread crumbs. Season with salt and pepper to taste. Add the scallion and herbs, stir to mix, and pour over the artichoke hearts.

6. Bake for 25 minutes, or until lightly browned.

Per serving: 12 grams carbohydrates, 7 grams protein, 1.5 grams fat

---

Zone Tip
Carbohydrates that have a high-glycemic index can cause a higher production of insulin if eaten by themselves without protein to balance them. Higher production of insulin results in the body not only storing more fat but also burning less fat. Carbohydrates that fall into this category are sugar, bread, cake, potatoes, pasta, and rice.

Lettuce Wraps with Thai Peanut Sauce

Taking a page from Southeast Asian cooking, I serve this peanutty turkey-vegetable mixture wrapped in lettuce. The texture is deliciously crunchy, and the flavor is delightfully cool against the spiciness of the sauce. You can even put the turkey mixture on the table and let guests roll their own wraps. If you prefer, use mild whitefish or chicken instead of turkey. Just great with a glass of white wine!

Serves 6

3 tablespoons store-bought peanut sauce*
1 tablespoon sake or white wine
½ teaspoon arrowroot or cornstarch
1 tablespoon olive oil
1 carrot, cut into julienne
1 zucchini, cut into julienne
1 cup snow peas, sliced diagonally into thin strips
½ pound turkey breast meat, cut into thin strips
1 cup bean sprouts
4 scallions, sliced diagonally, white and green parts
12 large leaves Boston or Bibb lettuce

1. In a small bowl, whisk together the peanut sauce, sake, and arrowroot.

2. In a nonstick skillet, heat the olive oil over medium-high heat. Add the carrot, zucchini, and snow peas, and stir-fry for about 1 minute. Lift the vegetables from the skillet and set aside.

3. Add the turkey to the skillet and stir-fry for about 10 minutes, until cooked through. Return the vegetables to the skillet, add the sprouts and scallions, and stir well.

4. Add the peanut sauce to the skillet and stir-fry for about 1 minute, or until the sauce thickens slightly.

5. Divide the mixture among the lettuce leaves and roll each into a bundle. Secure with toothpicks, if necessary, and serve.

Per serving (2 wraps): 6 grams carbohydrates, 2 grams protein, 2.3 grams fat

*I like San-J-Peanut Sauce, which is available at most markets in the Asian food section. It's relatively low in carbohydrates, and I calculated the nutritional analysis based on using it in this recipe.

Zone Tip
Keep a log to track your diet and exercise. Studies have shown that doing so, and charting your progress along the way, can help you stay focused and motivated.

Shrimp Seviche Cocktail

The first time I made this was on Super Bowl Sunday when my beloved Patriots won the game. It was a thrilling day for us, and I was so pleased these shrimp matched the mood of the evening. Absolutely everyone loved them! I soak the shrimp in a lot of sauce, but you don't eat it all. In fact, you could probably add another 1 to 1½ pounds of shrimp to the mix to increase the number of servings. I like to use about 4 shrimp for each serving.

Serves 6

1 pound large or jumbo shrimp, peeled and deveined
¾ cup fresh lime juice
½ cup chopped yellow onion
1 cup peeled and chopped cucumber
½ cup ketchup*
⅓ cup chopped fresh cilantro
2 tablespoons hot red pepper sauce
1 tablespoon olive oil
½ teaspoon sea salt

1. In a glass, ceramic, or other nonreactive dish, combine the shrimp and lime juice. Stir gently to coat, cover the dish, and refrigerate for 1 hour to marinate.

2. Put the chopped onion in a colander and rinse well under cool running water. Drain and transfer to a mixing bowl. Add the cucumber, ketchup, cilantro, hot sauce, olive oil, and salt. Stir well and chill for about 10 minutes.

3. Lift the shrimp from the lime juice and divide them among six small plates. Spoon the cucumber-onion sauce on top of the shrimp and serve immediately.

Per serving: 6 grams carbohydrates, 11 grams protein, 2.3 grams fat

*I recommend Healthy Choice ketchup, which has only 16 grams of carbohydrates per serving. If selecting a different brand, check the labels and buy the one with the lowest carbohydrate count.

Flash-Cooked Seviche with Mushroom and Avocado

I love this appetizer, and no more than during the winter holidays, when so much of the food we serve is laden with carbohydrates. What a nice change this seafood salad is! I call it seviche, although it's not entirely accurate. Instead of "cooking" the squid and shrimp in an acidic marinade, as you would for authentic seviche, I cook them beforehand and then soak them in a lemony garlic dressing. Three tablespoons of olive oil may sound like a lot for a Zone-friendly recipe, but much of it drips off when the squid and shrimp are lifted from the dressing, and you can monitor how much of the remainder you spoon over the salad. And besides, a little extra fat will not affect your insulin levels and take you out of the Zone.

Serves 4

½ pound cleaned squid, cut crosswise into ¼-inch rings
¾ pound large shrimp, peeled and deveined
½ cup fresh lemon juice
3 tablespoons olive oil
2 tablespoons finely chopped flat-leaf parsley
1 tablespoon finely chopped cilantro
1 large garlic clove, minced
1 jalapeño pepper, seeded and minced
½ pound small mushrooms, thinly sliced
Sea salt and freshly ground pepper
2 navel oranges
2 firm, ripe Hass avocados, cut into ½-inch wedges

1. Fill two saucepans halfway with water and bring each to a boil over medium-high heat. Set a bowl of ice and water near the stove.

2. Put the squid in one saucepan and the shrimp in the other. Cook the squid for 1 minute. Cook the shrimp for about 3 minutes, until it turns pink. Drain the seafood and immediately submerge it in the ice water for about 2 minutes until cool. Drain and pat dry.

3. In a large bowl, combine the lemon juice, olive oil, parsley, cilantro, garlic, and jalapeño. Add the mushrooms, shrimp, and squid and toss gently. Season with salt and pepper and refrigerate for about 10 minutes to chill.

4. Using a sharp knife, peel the oranges, removing all the bitter white pith. Working over a bowl to catch the juice, cut the fruit into sections. Pour the collected juice into the bowl with the seafood.

5. Arrange the orange sections and avocado wedges around the outside of a platter. Using a slotted spoon, pile the seviche in the center of the platter, and spoon some of the marinade over the oranges and avocados. Serve immediately.

Per serving: 14 grams carbohydrates, 25 grams protein, 12 grams fat

Frozen Strawberry Margaritas

When the weather turns warm in Massachusetts, everyone spends as much time outdoors as possible, and grilling is one of our favorite pastimes. I usually serve these margaritas with the Grilled Shrimp on page 57 for a super outdoor party and a meal that stays firmly in the Zone. You may want to serve them with something else that balances the drink just as well. A traditional margarita has nearly 100 grams of carbohydrates, while mine has only 18. And it's just as tasty! All you need is a blender with the ability to chop ice.

Serves 4

1½ cups slightly thawed frozen strawberries
⅓ cup freshly squeezed lime juice (3 to 4 limes)
⅓ cup tequila (80 proof)
⅓ cup Cointreau
Ice
3 tablespoons Splenda, optional

1. In a blender, combine the strawberries, lime juice, tequila, and Cointreau. Add enough ice to fill the blender. Cover and blend until thick and smooth and all the ice is crushed. Taste and sweeten with Splenda, if necessary.

2. Pour into margarita glasses and serve.

Per serving: 18 grams carbohydrates, 0 grams protein, 0 grams fat

Grilled Shrimp

This marinade does not have acid and so will not "cook" the shrimp before you get them to the grill. But it will provide subtle flavor that can't be beat, with enough garlic to stand up to the Frozen Strawberry Margaritas on page 56. To round out this meal, add some steamed vegetables.

Serves 4

4 garlic cloves, chopped
¼ cup chopped fresh cilantro or flat-leaf parsley
1 tablespoon olive oil
⅛ teaspoon sea salt

Freshly ground pepper
1 pound extra-large or jumbo shrimp, peeled and deveined
Olive oil cooking spray

1. In a glass, ceramic, or rigid plastic bowl, combine the garlic, cilantro, olive oil, and salt. Stir, and season to taste with pepper.

2. Add the shrimp, cover, and refrigerate for 1 hour.

3. Prepare a charcoal or gas grill. Lightly coat the grill rack with olive oil cooking spray. The coals or heating elements are ready when they are medium-hot. Alternatively, preheat a countertop grill.

4. Lift the shrimp from the marinade and let the liquid drip back into the bowl. Thread the shrimp on skewers or lay them in a grilling basket and grill for about 2 minutes on each side, or until they turn pink and are cooked through. Serve right away.

Per serving: 1 gram carbohydrates, 23 grams protein, 3.5 grams fat

Shrimp Crisps

When you want to make a splash at a party, serve these little cups filled with a tasty shrimp-and-peanut mixture. Impressive and pretty, they taste fantastic! Take care when you lift the little cups from the baking tin, and let them cool completely before filling them. Don't let them sit too long before serving, or the cups could get a little soggy.

Serves 4

Olive oil cooking spray
12 wonton or round wraps, about 3¼ inches in diameter
⅔ cup chopped cooked shrimp (about ¾ pound shrimp)
⅔ cup packaged coleslaw mix
2 tablespoons chopped unsalted peanuts
2 tablespoons hoisin sauce
Hot sauce

1. Preheat the oven to 400°F.

2. Invert a mini muffin tin with at least ten cups on a baking sheet. Lightly coat the bottom with olive oil cooking spray. Drape each muffin cup with a wonton wrapper, pressing the wrappers against the molds so that each one will form a little cup when baked.

3. Bake for 4 minutes, or until the wonton cups are lightly browned.

4. Let the wonton cups cool for about 1 minute and then carefully lift them off the molds and set them upright on wire racks for about 30 minutes until completely cooled.

5. Meanwhile, in a large bowl, combine the shrimp, coleslaw, peanuts, and hoisin sauce. Season to taste with hot sauce.

6. When the cups are cool, fill each one with the shrimp mixture. Serve as soon as possible.

Per serving: 12 grams carbohydrates, 17 grams protein, 2 grams fat

Zone Tip
Make a list of what you hope to achieve when you decide to try the Zone lifestyle. Check each goal off as you accomplish it—losing a few pounds, walking a mile, cutting out pasta—and add more as you go along. One goal a week is about right.

Hoisin Chicken in Endive

Few appetizers are easier or look more elegant than these endive leaves stuffed with boldly flavored chicken. The chicken salad on its own is a treat, served with butter lettuce or by itself. This is very low in carbohydrates—have a glass of wine with it!

Serves 6

⅔ cup chopped cooked chicken
⅔ cup coleslaw mix
2 tablespoons hoisin sauce
1 tablespoon chopped macadamia nuts
Hot red pepper sauce
2 whole heads Belgian endive, rinsed and cored

1. In a large bowl, toss the chicken with the coleslaw. Add the hoisin sauce, nuts, and hot sauce to taste and toss again.

2. Peel the endive into six individual leaves. Trim the ends if necessary.

3. Spoon a little chicken onto each endive leaf. Arrange on a platter and serve.

Per serving: 5 grams carbohydrates, 9 grams protein, 3.6 grams fat

Zone Tip

Know basic food storage and safety. Keep raw and cooked foods separate, and keep hot foods hot and cold foods cold. Harmful bacteria will grow most readily at room temperature. Wash your hands, utensils, and cutting boards frequently and thoroughly with warm water and soap. This is particularly important when you're working with raw poultry and meat.

Stuffed Mushrooms

I make these stuffed mushrooms often, particularly during the holidays when I may be tempted to leave the Zone. I readily admit it's hard to "zone" your way through a series of lavish parties, but if you remain aware of what you eat, you won't fall victim to the 5- to 8-pound weight gain so many Americans experience in December. Here's an idea: Make a platter of these mushrooms and take them with you to the next party. Not only are they yummy, but also they are Zone favorable.

Serves 4

1 pound large, white stuffing mushrooms (about 16), cleaned*
Juice of half a lemon
2 garlic cloves
1 shallot, peeled
1 tablespoon whole wheat bread crumbs
¼ cup shredded soy mozzarella or jalapeño soy mozzarella cheese
2 teaspoons low-sodium tamari (See note on page 136 about
    tamari.)
2 teaspoons tahini

1. Preheat the oven to 350°F.

2. Remove and reserve the mushroom stems. Dip the mushroom caps in lemon juice to prevent discoloration and set aside.

3. In a food processor fitted with the metal blade, process the garlic, shallot, and mushroom stems just until chopped, not pureed.

4. Add the bread crumbs, cheese, tamari, and tahini. Pulse until well mixed and moistened.

5. Using a spoon, fill the mushroom caps with the cheese mixture, dividing it evenly among them. Transfer the mushrooms to a nonstick baking sheet and bake for 20 minutes, or until the filling browns and turns a little crispy.

Per serving (4 mushrooms): 5 grams carbohydrates, 1 gram protein, 4.5 grams fat

*Clean mushrooms with a brush or paper towel rather than rinsing them under running water to prevent them from absorbing moisture.

Stuffed Portobello Mushrooms

One of these mushrooms serves as a satisfying and elegant first course, but it could also be part of a light lunch. For smaller hors d'oeuvres, stuff the vegetable mixture into smaller white mushrooms. I recommend whole wheat bread crumbs, which taste just as good as other bread crumbs, do the job of binding the filling, and are a more healthful carbohydrate. This is exactly the kind of "trick" that makes many of your favorite dishes more Zone friendly.

Serves 4

Olive oil cooking spray
2 teaspoons olive oil
½ cup finely chopped yellow onion
¼ cup finely chopped red bell pepper
¼ cup finely chopped green bell pepper
2 garlic cloves, chopped
1 cup nonfat or low-fat cottage cheese

¼ cup grated pepper Monterey Jack soy cheese or low-fat pepper
  Monterey Jack cheese
2 teaspoons Worcestershire sauce
¼ cup dried whole wheat Italian-flavored bread crumbs
4 portobello mushrooms, stems and dark gills removed
½ teaspoon paprika
3 tablespoons grated soy Parmesan or low-fat Parmesan cheese

1. Preheat the oven to 350°F. Coat a shallow baking dish large
enough to hold the mushrooms in a single layer with olive oil
cooking spray.

2. In a nonstick skillet, heat the olive oil over medium-high heat.
Sauté the onion, bell peppers, and garlic for about 5 minutes, or until
tender. Add the cottage cheese, Jack cheese, and Worcestershire
sauce, reduce the heat to medium-low, and stir gently until the
cheese melts.

3. Remove the skillet from the heat and add the bread crumbs. Stir
until blended. The mixture will be thick.

4. Spoon the cheese-and-vegetable mixture onto the stem-side of
the mushroom caps, dividing it evenly among them. Transfer the
filled mushrooms to the baking dish.

5. Bake for about 10 minutes, or until the mushrooms are tender
and the filling is heated through. Sprinkle with paprika and
Parmesan and serve immediately.

Per serving: 17 grams carbohydrates, 5 grams protein, 4 grams fat

Artichoke Hearts with Capers and Onion Spread

As a spread for rye crisps or as a chunky dip for raw vegetables, this treat is just as good in the winter as in the summer because it can be served either at room temperature or warm. It's also tasty alongside baked or poached fish. If you halve the artichoke hearts or leave them whole, this could be served as an appetizer on its own, with the artichoke hearts forming its base.

Makes about 2 cups

1 9-ounce package frozen artichoke hearts or 8.5-ounce can
1 tablespoon olive oil
1 small red onion, thinly sliced and quartered
½ red bell pepper, chopped
1 large garlic clove, minced
1 tablespoon drained capers
½ teaspoon Italian seasoning, or 1 tablespoon each chopped fresh
    oregano, flat-leaf parsley, and basil
Sea salt and freshly ground black pepper
½ teaspoon Herbamare

1. Cook the artichoke hearts according to the package directions. Drain in a colander and allow to cool.

2. Meanwhile, in a large nonstick frying pan, heat the olive oil over medium-high heat. Sauté the onion, bell pepper, and garlic for about 5 minutes, or until softened. Transfer to a food processor fitted with the metal blade.

3. Add the capers and seasoning (add artichoke at this time if making the spread) to the food processor and pulse until coarsely textured but spreadable. You should be able to see small pieces of

the ingredients. Stir and season to taste with salt, black pepper, and Herbamare. Serve warm or at room temperature.

Per 2 tablespoons: 31 grams carbohydrates, 0 grams protein, 1.4 grams fat

Hummus-in-the-Zone

Once you taste hummus made with ume paste, you will never make it any other way. The pungent, salty seasoning punches up the familiar spread for a marvelous fusion of Asian and Middle Eastern flavors. I use hummus in place of mayonnaise when I make chicken, turkey, or egg salad. I also fill hard-cooked egg whites with it for an easy snack that combines fat and carbohydrates (the hummus) with pure protein (the egg whites). If you prefer spicier hummus, sprinkle in a little more cayenne.

Makes about 2½ cups

1 19-ounce can chick-peas (garbanzo beans), drained and rinsed
3 to 4 garlic cloves, crushed
¼ red onion
¼ cup tahini
¼ cup fresh lemon juice
1 tablespoon ume paste*
Dash of cayenne

1. In a food processor fitted with the metal blade, process the chick-peas, garlic, onion, tahini, lemon juice, and ume paste until smooth.

2. Taste and season with cayenne.

Per 2 tablespoons: 5 grams carbohydrates, 1 gram protein, 2 grams fat

*Ume paste, also called umeboshi paste, is made from salted, pickled umeboshi plums. Often used in place of salt for seasoning, it's sold in Asian markets and some natural food stores.

Guacamole

I have a friend in Mexico City who taught me how she makes guacamole and explained how it's made differently throughout Mexico, with regional and personal variations everywhere you go. The most important ingredient is the avocado, which should be ripe enough to give evenly in your hand when you squeeze it gently. Ripe avocados are very dark and slightly soft to the touch. For my money, the best-tasting ones are the bumpy, pear-shaped Hass avocados from California. Tomatoes and lime juice are also used in most versions, but otherwise, you can customize guac to your taste. I like a little kick, so I add the jalapeño, but feel free to omit it if you don't like the heat.

Makes about 1¼ cups

2 ripe Hass avocados
1 tablespoon finely chopped yellow onion
¼ small jalapeño pepper, finely chopped
¼ tomato, diced small
1 tablespoon finely chopped cilantro
2 tablespoons lime juice
Sea salt and freshly ground pepper
Herbamare

1. Peel the avocados and scrape the flesh into a bowl. Mash with a fork until smooth.

2. Add the onion, jalapeño, tomato, cilantro, and lime juice. Mix gently and season to taste with salt, pepper, and Herbamare.

Per 2 tablespoons: 2 grams carbohydrates, 0 grams protein, 3 grams fat

Lentil Soup

Lentil soup is one of the best warmer-uppers going. I make a big pot and freeze what we don't eat right away. This way, if the snow starts to fall before I get home, I remember what waits for me in the freezer and feel a little more comfortable.

When you make this soup, you don't need to do much tending once it's in the pot and simmering. In fact, you should not stir the soup while it cooks—just let the wakame do its thing. This sea vegetable softens the fibers of the other ingredients during cooking, which is useful to remember when you make any legume dish. Wakame, which turns green when it cooks, is rich in trace minerals, potassium, and fiber. I chop the vegetables in a food processor so that the pieces are small, which is how I like them, although you may prefer yours a little larger. For a ZonePerfect meal, serve this soup with chicken and steamed vegetables dressed with just a little olive oil.

Serves 16; makes about 24 cups

4 dried wakame strands, broken into small pieces
1 large white onion, chopped
4 carrots, peeled or scrubbed, chopped

3 parsnips, peeled and chopped
3 ribs celery, halved lengthwise and chopped
3 cups green, brown, or red lentils, rinsed
Herbamare
White pepper
3 scallions, white and green parts, sliced diagonally
1 cup chopped flat-leaf parsley

1. In a small bowl, soak the wakame in enough cool tap water to cover it by about 1 inch for 15 minutes. The seaweed will swell.

2. In an 8-quart stockpot, layer the onion, carrots, parsnips, celery, and lentils. Add the wakame and soaking water. Add enough water to cover the lentils and vegetables by 3 inches. Bring the pot to a boil over high heat, reduce the heat to low, and simmer for about 1 hour.

3. Season with Herbamare and add pepper to taste. Stir and simmer for about 10 minutes longer; taste and adjust the seasonings. (I usually use at least 2 tablespoons of Herbamare and ½ teaspoon pepper.)

4. Ladle the soup into bowls and garnish with scallion slices and parsley.

5. To store, pour the soup into 16-ounce containers, cover tightly, and refrigerate for up to 10 days or freeze for up to 6 months.

Per serving: 16 grams carbohydrates, 0 grams protein, 0 grams fat

Zone Tip

When you go through a buffet or are at a cocktail party, take a small plate, and when you've filled it with food that is the most Zone favorable, walk away. This isn't the last buffet you will eat! Make sure that you get enough protein and that two-thirds of the plate is fruits and vegetables. Get involved with socializing with those around you so your focus is off of food.

Sweet-and-Sour Soup

When the cold Massachusetts winds blow, I like to cozy up with a piping hot bowl of soup. This is one of my mom's recipes, and so it nourishes my spirit as well as my body. Nothing tastes better! The piquant sweet-and-sour broth bathes the vegetables in perfect harmony, and the soup freezes beautifully. For more protein, add a little cooked turkey or chicken meat to make a complete meal.

Serves 8; makes about 12 cups

1½ pounds short ribs, trimmed of all excess fat
1 turkey wing
1 yellow onion, cut into thick chunks or rings
3 small beets, cut into eighths
2 large, firm sweet apples, such as Gala or Fuji, peeled and coarsely chopped
1 14-ounce can tomatoes
1 large head cabbage (about 2¾ pounds), quartered and cut into chunks
¾ cup fresh lemon juice
¾ cup Splenda
Sea salt

1. In a stockpot, bring 2 quarts of water and short ribs to a boil over medium-high heat. Skim the foam that rises to the surface. Add the turkey wing and onion, and reduce the heat to medium-low so that the liquid simmers. Add the beets, apple, and tomatoes. Partially cover and cook at a gentle simmer for about 90 minutes or until the meat is tender. Using a slotted spoon, discard as much of the onion as possible. Lift the meat from the pot with a slotted spoon and set aside to cool.

2. Cut the cabbage quarters into chunks and transfer to a microwave-safe bowl. Cover with plastic wrap and microwave at

High power for 2 minutes or until softened. Check the cabbage and add about ½ cup of water to moisten, if needed. Stir and microwave for 2 to 4 minutes longer or until softened. Drain any liquid that has accumulated in the bowl and add the cabbage to the soup.

3. Pull the beef and turkey off the bones and return the meat to the soup. Let the soup simmer for about 15 minutes. Add the lemon juice and Splenda, and season to taste with salt. Stir and adjust the seasoning.

Per serving: 17 grams carbohydrates, 13 grams protein, 9 grams fat

Gerdy's Vegetable Soup

My dear friend Gerdy makes a wonderful, rich-tasting vegetable soup, which is especially appealing to garlic lovers (like me!), and I couldn't write a book without including it. Luckily, many supermarkets sell whole, peeled garlic cloves in the produce aisle, which makes this recipe easier than ever to prepare. The soup takes 1½ hours to cook, but because it does not need much attention, this shouldn't be a problem. You do have to prepare a lot of vegetables, but I suggest buying them already cut up, if you can, or using a food processor to chop some of them. This soup is great to have in the wintertime in place of salad.

Serves 12

Olive oil spray
3 sweet onions, such as Vidalia, thinly sliced
2 8-ounce packages white mushrooms, cleaned and sliced
36 to 40 garlic cloves, peeled and left whole

4 red bell peppers, or a mixture of yellow, orange, and red bell
   peppers, seeded and diced
2 pounds carrots, peeled and coarsely chopped
1 pound parsnips, peeled and coarsely chopped
1 pint grape tomatoes
1 pound string beans, trimmed and halved if long
2 yellow summer squash, sliced about ¼ inch thick
2 zucchini, sliced about ¼ inch thick
Herbamare and freshly ground pepper
Large handful of chopped flat-leaf parsley

1. In an 8-quart pot lightly coated with olive oil spray, sauté the
onions, mushrooms, and garlic cloves over low heat for about 5
minutes, stirring, or until the mushrooms release their juices.

2. Add the peppers, carrots, parsnips, tomatoes, and enough water
to fill the pot to about 1½ inches from the rim. Bring to a boil over
medium-high heat, reduce the heat, and simmer for about 1 hour.

3. Add the string beans and simmer for 15 minutes longer. Add the
squash and zucchini, and simmer for about 15 minutes or until
tender. Season to taste with Herbamare and pepper. Ladle into bowls
and serve garnished with parsley.

Per serving: 15 grams carbohydrates, 0 grams protein, 0 grams fat

Variation
Add ¼ cup of hot, cooked white, kidney, garbanzo, or black beans
and you will add 9 grams of carbohydrates per serving. If you add
¾ pound of squeezed, cubed tofu, or 4 ounces of shredded, cooked
chicken, you will add 28 grams of protein, which makes this a Zone-
favorable meal along with a salad and fruit for dessert.

Shrimp Soup with Ginger and Snow Peas

Try this on a cold winter evening, and you won't mind the frigid temperatures outside. Just the flavor of the ginger alone leaves you with a warm glow that is so reassuring on long, dark nights. The soup can be prepared in an hour or made a day ahead. If you make it in advance, don't add the eggs until you reheat it for serving. To turn this into a complete Zone meal, add a cup of cooked brown rice to the soup and serve it with the Arugula and Kidney Bean Salad, page 82, and a half cup of cubed fresh pineapple.

Serves 6

1¼ pounds large unshelled shrimp (24/30 count)
1 teaspoon olive oil
1 yellow onion, quartered
1 carrot, quartered
1 rib celery with leaves, quartered
2 plum tomatoes, quartered
5 sprigs flat-leaf parsley
½ teaspoon hot red chili paste or garlic chili paste
1 tablespoon freshly grated ginger
2 garlic cloves, minced
1 bay leaf
¼ pound snow peas, halved diagonally
Herbamare and freshly ground pepper
2 large eggs, lightly beaten

1. Peel the shrimp and reserve the shells.

2. In a large saucepan, heat the olive oil over medium heat and cook the onion, carrot, and celery, stirring often, for 4 minutes, or until

the vegetables begin to soften. Add the tomatoes and parsley, and cook for 3 minutes longer.

3. Stir in the chili paste, ginger, garlic, bay leaf, and shrimp shells. Add 2 quarts water. Bring the contents to a boil, and then lower the heat to medium and simmer for about 20 minutes, or until the vegetables are tender and the flavors blended.

4. Strain through a sieve into a clean saucepan, pressing on the solids to extract as much of the flavor as possible. Discard the solids.

5. Add the snow peas to the saucepan, and cook over medium heat so that the liquid simmers. Add the shrimp and cook for about 2 minutes longer, or until the shrimp turn pink. Season to taste with Herbamare and pepper. Remove the pot from the heat.

6. Add the beaten eggs by swirling them in a thin stream over the hot soup. Stir the soup gently with a fork so that the eggs form strands.

7. Spoon the soup into bowls and serve.

Per serving: 5 grams carbohydrates, 21 grams protein, 4.4 grams fat

Gazpacho

Gazpacho has a long and honored history as the queen of uncooked soups and, as such, is especially welcoming in the hot summer months. It's not surprising that it can trace its roots to sunny Spain, where the tomatoes turn plump and juicy in the sunshine, garlic grows with abandon, and other vegetables traditionally used in the soup are beautiful. I add shrimp for protein and extra interest. I love this Zone-friendly soup and tend to make sizable batches and eat it all summer long.

Serves 4; makes about 1 quart

1 teaspoon olive oil
½ cup finely chopped mushrooms
1½ cups tomato juice, or ¼ cup tomato paste mixed with 1¼ cups
  water
½ pound small cooked shrimp
1 cup finely chopped tomato
¾ cup finely chopped green or red bell pepper
½ cup finely chopped yellow onion
½ cup finely chopped celery
½ cup finely chopped cucumber
¼ cup herbed vinegar, such as thyme, sage, or tarragon
¼ cup fresh whole-grain bread crumbs
1 garlic clove, crushed
1 tablespoon fresh lime juice
2 teaspoons minced flat-leaf parsley
1 teaspoon snipped chives
Hot red pepper sauce

1. In a small skillet, heat the olive oil over medium-high heat and sauté the mushrooms for 3 to 4 minutes, or until they soften and exude moisture. Add a few drops of water in the first minutes of cooking to prevent sticking.

2. In a large bowl, combine the remaining ingredients. Stir in the mushrooms. Cover and refrigerate for at least 2 hours, or until chilled.

Per serving: 19 grams carbohydrates, 12 grams protein, 2 grams fat

Spinach Gazpacho

With a little forethought, you can keep a bowl of this simple and tasty soup in the refrigerator all week long. What a great snack or addition to a meal! To do so, make the soup without the sour cream and then stir in the cream just before serving (about 2 teaspoons per bowl). If you want more egg in each bowl, hard-cook 16 eggs, discard the yolks, and chop up the whites.

Serves 8; makes about 14 cups

Juice of 1½ lemons
1 pound frozen chopped spinach, partially thawed
6 tablespoons nonfat sour cream
2 teaspoons sea salt
1 teaspoon freshly ground pepper
8 scallions, white and green parts, sliced (1 per bowl)
16 radishes, sliced
1 cup diced cucumber (2 heaping tablespoons per bowl)
8 hard-cooked eggs, sliced

1. In a large pot, bring 7 cups water and the lemon juice to a boil over medium-high heat. Stir in the spinach, return the contents to a boil, and remove from the heat. Let the soup cool, and then refrigerate it for at least 1 hour, or until cold.

2. Dip a ladle into the cold soup and remove 2 cups of broth, with as little spinach as possible, and transfer it to a bowl. Stir the sour cream into the bowl until smooth. Return the mixture to the pan, and season with salt and pepper.

3. Ladle the soup into eight bowls and garnish each with the scallions, radishes, cucumber, and eggs.

Per serving: 7 grams carbohydrates, 8 grams protein, 5 grams fat

Cucumber Salad

Cucumbers are practically nothing but water, so it's not surprising that this is a refreshing summer salad and one that tastes cool and wonderful with grilled chicken or fish. I use garden-variety cucumbers or long, seedless European cucumbers, which are also called English cucumbers. This recipe is one of the lowest in carbohydrates, so I consider it a freebie! Enjoy it anytime.

Serves 4

3 large cucumbers or 2 European cucumbers, peeled and thinly sliced
1 large red onion, thinly sliced
2 tablespoons snipped fresh chives
2 teaspoons snipped fresh dill
½ cup fresh lemon juice
¼ cup water
2 tablespoons Splenda
1 teaspoon sea salt
¼ teaspoon lemon pepper

1. In a mixing bowl, combine the cucumber, onion, chives, and dill.

2. In a small bowl, whisk together the lemon juice, water, Splenda, salt, and lemon pepper. Pour over the vegetables, toss well, and marinate for 15 to 30 minutes before serving.

Per serving: 9 grams carbohydrates, 0 grams protein, 0 grams fat

Zone Tip

Going to the grocery store or local gourmet market for your lunch can be fast and easy. Here are some easy options for lunch at the salad bar.

Eat as much as you want:

Alfalfa sprouts	Celery	Onions
Bean sprouts	Cucumbers	Radishes
Broccoli	Endive	Snow peas
Cabbage	Leafy greens	Spinach
Cauliflower	Mushrooms	

For 9 grams of carbohydrates, eat one serving of any of these:

8 or 9 slices red or green bell pepper (to equal approximately 1 whole pepper)

6 or 7 slices tomato (to equal approximately 1 whole tomato), or 5 or 6 cherry tomatoes

¼ cup lentils

¼ cup garbanzo beans

¼ cup hummus

½ apple

½ cup grapes

½ orange

For 28 grams of protein, eat one serving of the following:

¼ pound sliced turkey breast

¾ pound tofu

¼ pound tuna

1 ounce cheese plus 3 ounces turkey, shrimp, or tuna

1 cup cottage cheese

For 9 grams of fat:

1 tablespoon vinaigrette dressing

Arugula and Roasted Pear Salad

Hamersley's Bistro, which has been a mainstay of Boston's South End and one of my favorite spots for years, serves a roasted pear salad that I just adore. I adapted it to fit into the Zone as well as my home kitchen. The vegetarian bacon adds excellent flavor and makes this a nice first course before a low-protein main course.

Serves 4

4 slices vegetarian bacon
2 ripe pears, such as Anjou or Bartlett
Herbamare or sea salt
Freshly ground pepper
Olive oil cooking spray
2 ounces low-fat blue cheese, crumbled
2 tablespoons balsamic vinegar
1 teaspoon Dijon mustard
1 shallot, finely chopped
¼ cup olive oil
4 cups arugula
1 small red onion, thinly sliced

1. Preheat the oven to 350°F.

2. Fry the bacon in a skillet over medium-high heat until golden brown. Drain well on paper towels.

3. Cut each pear in half and remove the core. Sprinkle the cut sides with Herbamare and pepper.

4. Spray a skillet with olive oil cooking spray, and cook the pear halves, cut-sides down, over medium heat for 5 to 7 minutes, or until well browned.

5. Transfer the pears, cut-sides up, to a nonstick baking sheet (or one sprayed with olive oil cooking spray) and bake for 7 to 9 minutes, or until they are soft but not mushy.

6. Pull the baking sheet from the oven, and sprinkle the blue cheese over the pears; return the pears to the oven and bake 3 to 4 minutes longer, or until the cheese melts.

7. To make the dressing, in a small bowl, whisk together the vinegar, mustard, and shallot. Add the olive oil in a steady stream, whisking constantly until blended. Season to taste with Herbamare and pepper.

8. In a mixing bowl, combine the arugula and onion, and add enough dressing to moisten them. Reserve ⅓ to ½ cup of the dressing.

9. Divide the salad among four plates. Set a pear half on each one and drizzle some of the remaining dressing on top. Top each plate with a slice of bacon, and serve at once.

Per serving: 17 grams carbohydrates, 5 grams protein, 20 grams fat

Tuna and Apple Salad

How you serve this salad is up to you. For example, I like the texture of the apple once it's been warmed in the microwave, and I also like the lentils nice and warm. You might prefer a crisp, cool apple and room-temperature lentils. It's up to you, but any way you cut it, this is a refreshing and Zone-friendly lunch or supper salad.

Serves 1

1 firm tart apple, peeled and cut into chunks
1 cup mixed greens
3 ounces tuna packed in water, drained
¼ teaspoon drained capers
2 teaspoons olive oil
Juice of ½ lemon
Herbamare and freshly ground pepper
¼ cup warm, cooked lentils

1. In a microwave-safe bowl, microwave the apple at High for 1½ minutes, or until softened.

2. In a separate bowl, toss the greens with the tuna and capers. Add the apple. Dress with olive oil and lemon juice, and season to taste with Herbamare and pepper.

3. Put the salad on a plate and surround with lentils.

Per serving: 27 grams carbohydrates, 21 grams protein, 9 grams fat

Zone Tip

Attitude is *the* most important part of changing your lifestyle to the Zone. Having a positive attitude and knowing that this is the way you want to live the rest of your life will get you further than anything else. Studies have shown that when people believe they can change, they do.

Spinach Salad with Japanese Eggplant

I really like warm salads, even in the summertime, when I often serve this eggplant-and-spinach salad. The eggplant is cooked until soft, of course, but the bell peppers are cooked only slightly so that they retain their crunch. The vegetables, tossed with fresh spinach and dressed with a little lemon juice, taste divinely fresh and delicious. Japanese eggplant is long and skinny, with a lovely pale purple color. If you can't find it in your market, substitute a small purple or white eggplant.

Serves 2 as a main course, 4 as a side salad

2 teaspoons olive oil
1 yellow onion, sliced
1 garlic clove, crushed
3 Japanese eggplants, peeled and sliced into rounds
3 red bell peppers, cut into ¼-inch-thick strips
1 large bunch of baby spinach, thoroughly washed and dried
Juice of ½ lemon
4 ounces low-fat feta cheese, crumbled

1. In a wok or large frying pan, heat the olive oil over medium-high heat. Add the onion and garlic, and stir-fry for about 2 minutes. Add the eggplant and stir-fry for about 4 minutes, until tender. Add the bell pepper and stir-fry for about 2 minutes, so that it softens but remains crunchy.

2. In a large bowl, toss the spinach with the lemon juice and feta. Add the stir-fried vegetables, toss gently, and serve warm.

Per main course serving: 21 grams carbohydrates, 11 grams protein, 20 grams fat

Per side salad serving: 6 grams carbohydrates, 3 grams protein, 5.5 grams fat

---

Zone Tip

Weight training causes the body to release growth hormones. Not only do these hormones repair damage done to muscle tissue during exercise, but also they are among the most powerful fat-burning hormones in the body. I recommend you lift weights two or three times per week.

Arugula and Kidney Bean Salad

When you are deciding what to serve with fish, try this. What a tasty combination! And eating beans is a great way to ensure that you get enough fiber without having to munch 10 cups of lettuce for the same benefit. Beans are also a good source of protein with very little fat. Kidney beans are usually dark red, and I like the way the red beans look with the green arugula and red onions. But if you have only pink or white kidney beans, don't let that stop you from making this salad.

Serves 4

2 cups cooked or drained, canned red kidney beans*
½ cup finely chopped red onion
2 tablespoons chopped fresh basil
2 tablespoons olive oil
2 to 3 tablespoons red wine vinegar
Sea salt and freshly ground pepper
4 cups stemmed arugula, watercress, or mesclun mix
¼ cup shaved Parmesan or soy Parmesan cheese, optional

1. In a large bowl, combine the beans, onion, basil, and olive oil. Add 2 tablespoons of the vinegar and season to taste with salt and pepper. Taste and add more vinegar if necessary.

2. Arrange the arugula on a serving platter. Spoon the beans on top. Sprinkle with Parmesan, if using, and serve.

Per serving: 18 grams carbohydrates, 2 grams protein, 7 grams fat

*When I have time, I prefer to cook beans rather than use canned. Here's how: First, rinse them well, and then soak them in enough cold water to cover them by about an inch for at least six hours, or overnight. If you can, change the water once or twice during soaking. Drain the beans and put them in a large pot with enough cold water to cover them by a few inches. Add a piece of kombu as it comes in its package. Kombu is a seaweed that helps break down the enzymes in the beans and makes them easier to digest. This dark green sea vegetable is sold in most health food stores. Cook the beans and kombu at a simmer for 1 to 1½ hours, or until soft enough to squash between your fingers but not mushy. Check the water level during cooking and add more to keep the beans completely covered. Discard the kombu before serving.

Mesclun Greens with Roasted Red Peppers, Portobello Mushrooms, and Feta

I often add a little cheese to salads when I want to make something special or just feel in the mood for a taste of luxury. The contrast

here among the cool greens, the warm grilled vegetables, and the creamy feta cheese is fabulous. Be sure to make this when your outside grill is up and running. You won't be sorry!

Serves 6

6 large portobello mushrooms
¾ cup Balsamic Vinaigrette, page 99
3 roasted bell peppers, quartered*
3 tablespoons extra-virgin olive oil
1 tablespoon balsamic vinegar
1 garlic clove, roughly chopped
Vegetable oil cooking spray
1 tablespoon chopped flat-leaf parsley
6 cups mesclun mix or baby spinach greens, or combination of both
2 ounces feta cheese, crumbled

1. Remove the stems from the mushrooms and discard them. Clean the mushroom caps with a mushroom brush or damp cloth.

2. Put the mushrooms in a shallow glass, ceramic, or rigid plastic container. Pour ½ cup of the vinaigrette over them. Turn gently to coat. Cover and refrigerate for at least 6 hours and up to 24 hours.

3. In a glass, ceramic, or rigid plastic container, combine the roasted peppers, olive oil, vinegar, and garlic. Stir to mix. Cover and refrigerate for at least 1 hour and up to 36 hours.

4. Prepare a charcoal or gas grill. Lightly coat the grill rack with vegetable oil cooking spray. The coals or heating elements are ready when they are medium-hot. Alternatively, preheat a countertop grill.

5. Lift the mushrooms from the marinade and let the liquid drip back into the container. Discard the marinade. Grill the mushrooms, gill-side down, for about 5 minutes. Turn and grill for 3 to 5 minutes longer, or until softened and fragrant.

6. Remove the mushrooms from the grill and slice thinly.

7. Drain the peppers, discard their marinade, and dice the peppers.

8. In a large salad bowl, mix together the parsley, greens, peppers, mushrooms, and feta cheese. Dress with the remaining ¼ cup vinaigrette, toss, and serve.

Per serving: 8 grams carbohydrates, 2 grams protein, 17 grams fat

*To roast peppers, char them whole either under a preheated broiler, over a gas flame, or on a grill. Turn them as their skins blacken so that they char all over. This will take 7 to 10 minutes, depending on the size of the pepper and the amount of heat. Put the charred peppers in a paper bag and roll it closed, or place them in a bowl and cover with plastic wrap, and let them cool. When the peppers are cool enough to handle, rub the charred skin off (do not use water). Not every scrap of charred skin needs to be removed. Cut the peppers into quarters, and scrape out the seeds and ribs.

Zone Tip
Use extra-virgin olive oil to accent salads or vegetables that have already been cooked. While delicious as a salad dressing and in an uncooked preparation, extra-virgin olive oil is not a good choice for cooking. For cooking, use regular olive oil. This does not break down as readily as extra-virgin olive oil. It's less expensive than extra-virgin, too.

Warm Goat Cheese Salad

Looking for a special salad? I have had salads similar to this one at restaurants, but I like my version better. It's light and fruity because of the raspberries, and the crumbed slices of goat cheese add the indulgence that we all sometimes crave. This is a high-fat salad for the Zone, but extra fat does not affect insulin levels, so it's OK to treat yourself now and then. The rest of the meal should be low in fat.

Serves 6

Salad
6 cups mesclun greens or other baby greens
⅓ cup roughly chopped walnuts
3 ripe pears, such as Comice, Anjou, or Bartlett
4 ounces herbed or plain goat cheese
1 tablespoon fine, dried whole wheat bread crumbs
Olive oil cooking spray

Dressing
¼ pint raspberries
4 tablespoons olive oil
2 tablespoons raspberry vinegar
2 tablespoons mirin*
1 garlic clove, minced
Herbamare
Sea salt and freshly ground pepper

1. To assemble the salads, mound a cup of greens on each of six salad plates. Scatter about a tablespoon of walnuts over the greens on each plate.

2. Core the pears and slice them into thin wedges. Arrange the wedges around each salad, using about half a pear per serving.

3. Cut the goat cheese into six slices and lay them, cut-side up, on a cutting board. Sprinkle the top of the slices with half of the bread crumbs, and gently press the crumbs into the cheese. Turn the slices over and repeat with the remaining crumbs.

4. Coat a small nonstick skillet with a small amount of olive oil cooking spray. Put the cheese in the skillet and cook over medium-high heat for 1 minute. Turn, and cook 30 to 40 seconds longer, or until the cheese is about to melt. Place one slice on top of each salad.

5. To make the dressing, in a small bowl, mash the raspberries with a fork until roughly pureed. Transfer the puree to a jar. (You can process the raspberries in a food processor or blender for about a minute, if you prefer.)

6. Add the olive oil, vinegar, mirin, and garlic to the jar. Attach the lid, and shake to mix. Season to taste with Herbamare, salt, and pepper, and shake again. Pour about 2 tablespoons of dressing over each salad and serve.

Per serving: 17 grams carbohydrates, 4 grams protein, 22 grams fat

*Mirin is sweet rice wine with a very low alcohol content, usually less than 1 percent. It's sold in Asian markets, supermarkets, and specialty markets.

Jicama and Green Bean Salad with Sesame Vinaigrette

Jicama (pronounced HEE-kim-a) is a crisp, white-fleshed, Mexican root vegetable whose flavor lies midway between apple and potato. The haricot vert (a skinny French string bean) works best with this, but any slender green beans or even snow peas will also work. Mirin, a sweet rice seasoning, and black sesame seeds (if black sesame seeds aren't available, white ones will do) are used extensively in Japanese cooking.

Serves 4

Salad
Salt
½ pound haricots verts or other slender green beans, trimmed
1 pound jicama (1 small or ½ large jicama), peeled

Dressing
2 tablespoons mirin
1½ tablespoons rice vinegar
1 teaspoon toasted sesame oil
Sea salt and freshly ground pepper
2 teaspoons toasted sesame seeds or black sesame seeds (see page 167)

1. To make the salad, bring a 2-quart saucepan of lightly salted water to a boil. Add the beans and cook for 3 to 4 minutes, or until al dente. Drain the beans, rinse them under cold water, drain again, and then blot them dry with paper towels or a kitchen towel. Set aside to cool.

2. Cut the jicama into sticks about the size of the beans.

3. To make the dressing, in a salad bowl, whisk together the mirin, vinegar, and sesame oil. Season to taste with sea salt and pepper, and then whisk until the salt dissolves. Add the beans and jicama, and toss to mix. Taste and adjust the seasonings. Sprinkle with sesame seeds and serve.

Per serving: 4 grams carbohydrates, 0 grams protein, 4 grams fat

Salad Niçoise with Gloria's Vinaigrette Dressing

Salad Niçoise is a classic that too often is poorly prepared. Not mine! I take care to use small, tender potatoes; delicate, slender, crisp string beans; and the ripest, juiciest tomatoes I can find, to make the tuna-based salad sing a glorious Mediterranean song! I like anchovies, but if you want to omit them, do so. If you are an anchovy freak, add a few more, but keep in mind that each one adds a gram of protein.

Serves 4

½ pound small red potatoes, scrubbed but not peeled
½ pound slender string beans, trimmed*
6 cups red or green leaf lettuce, or a mixture of both, torn into
    large pieces
3 to 4 ripe tomatoes, quartered
3 hard-cooked eggs, peeled and quartered
2 anchovies, drained and patted dry and halved
12 pitted Niçoise olives
2 6-ounce cans water-packed tuna, drained and flaked
Gloria's Vinaigrette, page 98
Freshly ground pepper

1. Bring a large pot of water to a boil over medium-high heat. Add the potatoes, return to boiling, and cook for about 20 minutes, or until they're fork-tender. Drain the potatoes, rinse them under cold water, and allow them a few minutes to cool. When they're cool enough to handle, cut them into quarters and set them aside to cool completely.

2. In a large pot or steamer, steam the string beans in a steaming basket set over boiling water for 5 to 7 minutes, or until al dente. Drain, rinse with cold water, and set aside to cool.

3. Divide the lettuce among four salad plates. Build the salads by adorning the lettuce with the string beans, potatoes, tomatoes, eggs, anchovies, and olives.

4. Spoon tuna in the center of each salad and drizzle with 1 tablespoon of vinaigrette. Season with pepper and serve.

Per serving (without dressing): 18 grams carbohydrates, 26 grams protein, 2.5 grams fat

*For the most authenticity, buy slender string beans, which are also called haricots verts, French green beans, or filet beans. True haricots verts are expensive and often hard to find. So it's fine to substitute any fresh string beans, looking for the most slender ones you can find.

Zone Tip
Give yourself a massage once a month as a reward for doing well in the Zone. The massage will help to restore equilibrium and balance to your life. Barring a trip to the spa, take a long, luxurious bath every now and then!

Spinach and Fruit Salad

The dressing for this full-flavored and full-bodied salad is made with orange juice, which makes it just perfect to serve with duck, pheasant, turkey, or chicken. I love the interest the persimmon adds to the pear, jicama, and pecans.

Serves 6

Salad
12 cups fresh spinach or baby romaine
½ cup sliced jicama
1 Comice or Anjou pear, peeled and sliced
2 ripe Japanese or regular persimmons, seeds removed, sliced*
½ cup chopped, toasted pecans*

Dressing
¼ cup rice vinegar
6 tablespoons olive oil
6 tablespoons orange juice
2 small garlic cloves, minced
Sea salt and pepper

1. Divide the spinach among six salad plates. Top each with jicama, pear, and persimmon slices, and sprinkle with pecans.

2. In a small bowl, whisk together the vinegar, oil, orange juice, and garlic. Season to taste with salt and pepper.

3. Spoon 1 tablespoon of dressing over each salad and serve.

Per serving: 4 grams carbohydrates, 0 grams protein, 10 grams fat

*Persimmons, known as kakis in some countries, are available in the late fall through February. The brightly colored fruit with glossy, orange-red skin is an excellent source of vitamin A, a good source of vitamin C, and rich in fiber. Some persimmons have pointed ends, while others are rounded. Both should be plump and smooth, bright orange, and firm to the touch when you buy them. Let them ripen at room temperature until very soft. The fruit originated in China and then spread across Asia. Persimmons that grow in the United States can be traced to a Japanese variety. Today, most that are available to us grow in California.

To toast pecans, spread the shelled nuts in a pan in a single layer, and bake in a preheated 325°F oven for 10 to 12 minutes, stirring occasionally, until fragrant and lightly browned. Let the nuts cool before using.

Warm Salad with Crisp Tempeh Croutons

I was thrilled when I figured out how to make croutons from tempeh, which is made from fermented soybeans. Tempeh croutons are absolutely delicious and fill the need for bread croutons, which (let's face it) are rarely Zone friendly. Here, I serve the tempeh on top of wilted winter greens for a warm salad that appeals to everyone in the gray winter months. Too much fat here? Leave out the almonds—they're great, but you won't miss them too much.

Serves 2 as a main course, 4 as a side salad

Salad
1 8-ounce package tempeh, drained, halved lengthwise, and cut into
   1-inch cubes
Low-sodium tamari

3 cups chopped raw kale (1 bunch)
½ cup chopped watercress (1 bunch)
¼ cup slivered almonds, toasted*

Vinaigrette
2 tablespoons olive oil
2 tablespoons balsamic vinegar

1. Preheat the oven to 400°F.

2. To make the salad and croutons, in a small bowl, marinate the tempeh cubes in enough tamari to cover by a thin layer for at least 5 minutes and up to 1 hour.

3. Lift the tempeh from the marinade with a slotted spoon and spread it in a single layer in a glass baking dish (or metal baking pan that has been sprayed with vegetable oil cooking spray). Bake for about 30 minutes, or until crisp, turning once with a spatula. Cover to keep warm and set aside.

4. Meanwhile, in a steaming basket set over boiling water, steam the kale for 9 minutes, or until tender and wilted. Drain and transfer to a salad bowl.

5. Steam the watercress over boiling water for 2 to 3 minutes, or until tender and wilted. Drain and add to the kale. Sprinkle with the almonds, and toss to mix.

6. For the vinaigrette, in a small bowl, whisk the olive oil and vinegar. Drizzle over the greens and almonds, and toss. Top with the tempeh cubes and serve immediately.

Per main course serving: 18 grams carbohydrates, 16 grams protein, 11 grams fat

Per side salad serving: 9 grams carbohydrates, 8 grams protein, 5 grams fat

*To toast almonds, spread them in a small, dry skillet and cook over medium heat, shaking the pan occasionally for 5 to 8 minutes, or until lightly browned and fragrant.

Zone Tip

Keep your kitchen stocked with an adequate supply of onions, garlic, shallots, olive oil, balsamic vinegar, natural chicken broth, Dijon mustard, canned beans, and nuts. These are building blocks for healthful eating and cooking.

Lobster Salad

I include this recipe in the appetizer chapter because rich, expensive lobster does well served in small quantities. A little goes a long way, and this is a terrific start to a special-occasion meal. I don't think I have tasted a better lobster salad even along the coast of Maine. You can buy lobster meat already cooked, or you can steam two small lobsters to get enough claw and tail meat for the salad (and if there is a little extra, it won't hurt you!); just be sure the lobster meat is cold before you mix the salad.

Serves 2

1 rib celery, diced
1 tablespoon finely chopped yellow onion
1 tablespoon light mayonnaise or Nayonaise
Juice of ½ lemon
½ pound cooked lobster meat, cut into small pieces but not
    shredded
Herbamare
2 to 3 drops hot sauce, optional
4 slices avocado, for garnish
Chopped flat-leaf parsley, for garnish

1. In a small bowl, stir together the celery, onion, mayonnaise, and lemon juice. Add the lobster meat and mix gently to coat. Season to taste with Herbamare and hot sauce, if using. Mix well and adjust seasonings.

2. Spoon the lobster salad onto salad plates, garnish each with avocado and parsley, and serve.

Per serving: 5 grams carbohydrates, 21 grams protein, 6 grams fat

Israeli Chopped Salad

The addition of a pickle gives this salad an interesting flavor. If you lift the vegetables after they marinate and leave the dressing at the bottom of the bowl, you will save 3.5 grams of fat per serving. The analysis below reflects the amounts of carbohydrates, protein, and fat with the dressing.

Serves 2

2 Kirby (small, pickling) cucumbers, chopped
2 large tomatoes, chopped
1 green bell pepper, chopped
1 sour pickle, chopped
1 tablespoon extra-virgin olive oil
1 tablespoon fresh lemon juice
Sea salt and freshly ground black pepper

1. In a small, nonreactive bowl, mix together the cucumbers, tomatoes, bell pepper, and pickle. Add the olive oil and lemon juice, stir gently, and season to taste with salt and black pepper. Cover and refrigerate for at least 1 hour and up to 12 hours.

2. Serve cold or at room temperature.

Per serving: 9 grams carbohydrates, 0 grams protein, 7 grams fat

Jicama Slaw

Jicama is crisp, juicy, and sadly underused in much of the country. It's popular in the Southwest and throughout Mexico, and you also find it in many Asian dishes. Peel the tuber's thin skin to reveal the white flesh, which tastes good and adds crunch to this versatile, colorful slaw.

Serves 4

Slaw
1 to 1½ pounds thin-skinned jicamas, peeled and cut into julienne
1 red bell pepper, cut into julienne
1 yellow bell pepper, cut into julienne
1 orange bell pepper, cut into julienne
½ cup chopped fresh cilantro

Lemon vinaigrette
¼ cup fresh lemon juice
½ cup extra-virgin olive oil
Sea salt and freshly ground black pepper

1. To make the slaw, in a large bowl, toss together the jicama, bell peppers, and cilantro.

2. For the vinaigrette, in a small bowl, whisk together the olive oil and lemon juice. Season to taste with salt and black pepper, whisk, and pour over the slaw. Toss, and serve immediately.

Per serving: 10 grams carbohydrates, 0 grams protein, 9 grams fat

Tangy Coleslaw

In place of egg-based mayonnaise, I use Nayonaise, a soy product, which tastes great and is a better choice than light mayo. Look for it where the tofu is sold in most supermarkets and natural food stores. The dressing for the slaw is wonderful on steamed vegetables.

Serves 4

½ cup nonfat plain yogurt
2 tablespoons reduced-fat buttermilk
2 tablespoons Nayonaise
½ teaspoon Dijon mustard
1 small garlic clove, finely chopped
2 tablespoons chopped scallion, white and green parts
¼ teaspoon Herbamare or sea salt
Freshly ground pepper
1 20-ounce bag coleslaw mix*

1. In a bowl, whisk together the yogurt, buttermilk, Nayonaise, and mustard. Stir in the garlic, scallion, and Herbamare. Season to taste with pepper. Cover tightly and refrigerate for at least 1 hour and up to 12 hours.

2. When ready to serve, put the coleslaw mix in a large bowl. Pour the dressing over the mix and toss to coat. Serve immediately.

Per serving: 8 grams carbohydrates, 2 grams protein, 1.5 grams fat

*If you prefer, instead of using coleslaw mix, grate ½ head green cabbage, ½ head red cabbage, and 1 carrot.

Gloria's Vinaigrette

Here is another great salad dressing that I make often and never tire of. Use whatever fresh herb(s) you can get your hands on. You can't go wrong. This doubles as a wonderful marinade for lightly steamed and cooled vegetables. The recipe makes 1 cup, but I use only about 1 tablespoon per serving, which equals approximately 9 grams of fat.

Makes about 1 cup

¼ cup red wine vinegar
2 tablespoons finely minced shallot
1 to 2 tablespoons chopped fresh herbs, such as thyme, oregano,
    basil, or tarragon, or a mixture of these
2 teaspoons Dijon mustard
¾ cup extra-virgin olive oil
Sea salt and freshly ground pepper

1. In a small bowl, whisk together the vinegar, shallot, herbs, and mustard. Slowly whisk in the olive oil until blended. Season to taste with salt and pepper.

2. Use immediately or refrigerate in a lidded glass jar for up to a month. Shake or whisk before using.

Per 1 tablespoon: 0 grams carbohydrates, 0 grams protein, 9 grams fat

Balsamic Vinaigrette

This is one of my standard vinaigrettes; I find uses for it many times during the week. It's a classic and sure to become one of your favorites, too. Use the highest-quality olive oil and a low-acid balsamic vinegar (6 percent or lower) for the best flavor. I usually buy olive oil and vinegar at Trader Joe's.

Makes about 1 cup

¾ cup extra-virgin olive oil
¼ cup balsamic vinegar
¼ cup chopped flat-leaf parsley
1 teaspoon Herbamare or sea salt and pepper
1 garlic clove, crushed

1. In a small glass or ceramic bowl, whisk together the olive oil and vinegar. Add the parsley, Herbamare, and garlic. Whisk again, taste, and adjust the seasoning.

2. Store in a lidded container in the refrigerator for up to 1 month. Whisk before using.

Per 2 tablespoons: 1 gram carbohydrates, 0 grams protein, 17.5 grams fat

---

Zone Tip
Look for carbohydrate- and fat-free salad dressing at natural food markets and supermarkets. I like it not only for salads but also as a dipping sauce for raw vegetables. Try those made by Walden Farms, if you can find them.

$\mathcal{F}$ish and Seafood

101

Garlicky Grilled Shrimp

Although I grill these shrimp in a grilling basket to prevent them from falling through the grill rack, you could thread them on wooden or metal skewers instead. If you use wooden skewers, soak them for at least 20 minutes beforehand so that they don't scorch. This is a straightforward recipe for shrimp flavored with some of its best friends: garlic, olive oil, and cilantro.

Serves 4

4 garlic cloves, chopped
¼ cup chopped fresh cilantro or flat-leaf parsley
1 tablespoon olive oil
⅛ teaspoon sea salt
Freshly ground pepper
1 pound large shrimp, peeled and deveined (24/30 count)
Vegetable oil cooking spray

1. In a bowl, combine the garlic, cilantro, olive oil, salt, and pepper. Add the shrimp, toss to coat, cover, and refrigerate for at least 10 minutes and no longer than 2 hours.

2. Prepare a charcoal or gas grill so that the coals or heating elements are medium-hot. Coat a grilling basket with vegetable oil cooking spray.

3. Lift the shrimp from the marinade and lay them in the basket. Discard the marinade. Grill for 4 to 5 minutes, or until they turn pink. Serve immediately.

Per serving: 1 gram carbohydrates, 23 grams protein, 3.5 grams fat

Zone Tip

To avoid eating too quickly and thus eating too much, take time to enjoy your meal. Look at the food, and pay attention to the flavors, aromas, and textures. Your brain will tell you when to stop eating.

Chili-Garlic Shrimp

Shrimp is so great because it marries with just about any seductive flavor. Here, I pair it with chili-garlic sauce, oyster sauce, and a sprinkling of hot pepper flakes for a dish that gives your taste buds a pleasing workout. Serve this with green beans, baked spaghetti squash, and slices of fresh pineapple for a good Zone meal.

Serves 2

1½ tablespoons store-bought chili-garlic sauce
1½ tablespoons oyster sauce
1 teaspoon rice vinegar
2 teaspoons olive oil
3 garlic cloves
1 yellow onion, diced
½ red bell pepper, diced
½ green bell pepper, diced
½ pound medium shrimp, peeled and deveined (16/18 count)
6 to 8 dried hot red pepper flakes
½ teaspoon white pepper
¼ cup roasted cashews
2 scallions, white and green parts, sliced diagonally and chopped

1. In a small bowl, stir together the chili-garlic sauce, oyster sauce, and vinegar. Set aside.

2. In a medium sauté pan or wok, heat the olive oil over medium-high heat. Add the garlic and cook for 2 to 3 minutes, or until lightly browned. Add the onion and bell peppers and cook, stirring, for about 5 minutes, until the vegetables are softened. Take care the garlic does not burn.

3. Add the shrimp and cook, stirring occasionally, for 3 to 4 minutes, or until the shrimp begin to turn pink. Add the chili-garlic sauce mixture and the red pepper flakes, and cook 2 to 3 minutes longer, or until the shrimp are pink, opaque, and cooked through. Season with white pepper. Be sure not to overcook the shrimp.

4. Serve garnished with cashews and scallion.

Per serving: 8 grams carbohydrates, 24 grams protein, 6.5 grams fat

Zone Tip

Buy whole, peeled cloves of garlic from the supermarket and toss them in the bowl of a food processor fitted with the metal blade. Pulse just until chopped (not pureed) and then transfer the chopped cloves to a lidded glass jar. Drizzle a little olive oil over the chopped garlic, just enough to coat the surface with a film of oil. Cover tightly and refrigerate for up to 2 months. Chopped garlic, ready when you are!

Steamed Shrimp with Chinese Black Bean Sauce

The beauty of this black bean sauce is that it is equally fantastic with steamed fish or shrimp, baked tofu, or broiled chicken. And it's practically pure protein. Fermented black beans (also called salted or preserved), which are extremely salty and aromatic, are used in small amounts for a big punch. You can find them in Asian grocery stores, or in the Asian section of many supermarkets, packaged in small jars or plastic bags. This recipe makes enough sauce for four servings of shrimp, fish, tofu, or chicken, or any recipe with about a pound of protein.

Serves 4

2 tablespoons fermented black beans
2 garlic cloves, roughly chopped
2 teaspoons shredded or finely chopped fresh ginger
1 pound large shrimp, peeled and deveined (24/30 count)
3 tablespoons low-sodium tamari
2 tablespoons dry sherry
1½ teaspoons brown rice syrup or honey
2 scallions, green parts only, split lengthwise and cut into 1-inch
    pieces
Chopped fresh cilantro, for garnish

1. Pile the beans, garlic, and ginger on a large sheet of wax paper. Using the side of a cleaver or chef's knife, mash them into a rough paste.

2. Put the shrimp in a bowl, spoon the bean mixture over them, and toss to mix.

3. In a small bowl, combine the tamari, sherry, and brown rice syrup. Stir well, and pour over the shrimp.

4. Transfer the shrimp to a steaming basket and steam, tightly covered, over boiling water for about 5 minutes, or until the shrimp turn pink and are cooked through.

5. Serve garnished with scallions and cilantro.

Variations

Baked Fish with Black Bean Sauce: Preheat the oven to 350°F. Lightly coat a shallow baking dish with olive oil cooking spray. Lay a pound of cod, halibut, sole, or other mild whitefish fillets in the dish, spread the bean mixture over the fish, and pour the tamari mixture on top. Bake 20 to 30 minutes, depending on the thickness of the fish.

Baked Tofu with Black Bean Sauce: Follow the preceding instructions for Baked Fish with Black Bean Sauce, substituting a pound of sliced, firm tofu for the fish.

Broiled Chicken with Black Bean Sauce: Preheat the broiler. Lightly coat a shallow broiler pan with olive oil cooking spray. Lay a pound of boneless, skinless chicken breast halves in the pan, spread the bean mixture over the chicken, and pour the tamari mixture on top. Broil for 5 minutes, turn, and broil 5 to 6 minutes longer, or until cooked through.

Per serving (with shrimp): 10 grams carbohydrates, 24 grams protein, 0 grams fat

Zone Tip
If you have high levels of LDL in your blood profile and are struggling to bring them down, eat protein exclusively from fish, egg whites, and soy products. This diet, along with exercise, should help lower those "bad" cholesterol levels.

Greek Shrimp with Feta

It's the oregano and feta cheese that give this easy dish a Greek flair. I suggest low-fat feta, but if you prefer full-fat feta, cut the amount back to 2 ounces (if fat is not a problem for you, go for the full amount, since fat does not raise insulin levels). Serve some lovely, fresh steamed asparagus with this, and for additional carbs, have fruit for dessert.

Serves 4

2 teaspoons olive oil
1 pound medium shrimp, peeled and deveined (31/35 count)
2 garlic cloves, crushed
1 tablespoon minced fresh oregano, or ½ teaspoon dried
½ teaspoon sea salt
¼ teaspoon ground pepper
10 to 12 scallions (2 bunches), white and green parts, thinly sliced
3 tomatoes, coarsely chopped (about 1 pound)
4 ounces crumbled low-fat feta cheese

1. In a large nonstick frying pan, heat the olive oil over medium-high heat. Add the shrimp, garlic, oregano, salt, and pepper, and cook, stirring, for about 1 minute. Add the scallions and cook about 2 minutes longer, just until the shrimp are opaque.

2. Stir in the tomatoes and cook 3 to 4 minutes, until the tomatoes are heated through and softened and the shrimp are pink. Remove from the heat, sprinkle with feta cheese, and serve immediately.

Per serving: 4 grams carbohydrates, 25 grams protein, 3.5 grams fat

Shrimp Scampi with Sun-Dried Tomatoes

A mainstay of Italian restaurants, scampi is generally a meal of oil-and-garlic-doused shrimp served over pasta. My version is a little more Zone friendly, and while you could spoon it over pasta, it's not necessary. Eat it as it is, accompanied by a tossed salad. The sun-dried tomatoes are delicious with the shrimp. Be sure to soak the tomatoes beforehand so that they won't be tough.

Serves 4

2 tablespoons sun-dried tomatoes
2 teaspoons olive oil
1¼ pounds large shrimp, peeled and deveined (24/30 count)
¼ cup minced shallot
2 teaspoons minced garlic
¼ cup brandy or dry sherry
1 tablespoon fresh lemon juice
1 tablespoon minced fresh parsley or basil

1. Bring a small amount of water to a boil. Put the tomatoes in a small bowl, pour enough of the water over them to cover, and allow them to hydrate for about 20 minutes. Drain the tomatoes and chop them.

2. In a large frying pan, heat the olive oil over medium-high heat. Add the shrimp and cook, stirring, 2 to 3 minutes, or until the shrimp are pink on the outside and just a bit translucent in the center. Transfer the shrimp to a plate and cover to keep warm.

3. Put the shallot and garlic in the pan, and stir over medium-high heat for about 1 minute, until fragrant. Add the brandy, hydrated tomatoes, and lemon juice, and bring the contents to a boil. Reduce the heat and simmer for about 4 minutes, until the liquid reduces to about 1 tablespoon.

4. Remove the pan from the heat and stir in the parsley. Return the shrimp to the pan and toss to coat with the sauce. Cook, stirring, over medium heat for about 1 minute, just until the shrimp are heated through.

Per serving: 5 grams carbohydrates, 28 grams protein, 2.5 grams fat

Sea Scallops with Leeks

Because small Cape Cod and Maine scallops are harvested from late October until the end of January, I think of scallops as a wintry dish. If you're lucky enough to get freshly harvested Cape or Maine scallops, try them raw, and I promise they will practically melt in your mouth. Otherwise, buy the freshest, plumpest sea scallops you can find, and cook them with leeks, another wintertime treasure. Serve this dish with string beans, pea pods, or sugar snap peas, a quarter cup of brown rice, a salad, and a clementine for dessert.

Serves 2

2 teaspoons olive oil
2 leeks, white and light green parts, thinly sliced into rounds
1 tablespoon minced fresh ginger
1 garlic clove, crushed
⅓ cup dry white wine or dry vermouth
¾ pound sea or bay scallops
Sea salt and freshly ground pepper
¼ cup finely snipped chives

1. In a nonstick skillet, heat the olive oil over low heat. Add the leeks and cook, stirring, for about 8 minutes, until tender. Add the ginger and garlic, raise the heat to medium, and cook 2 minutes longer. Add the wine and bring the contents to a simmer.

2. Season the scallops with salt and pepper. Add them to the simmering wine, cover, reduce the heat to low, and cook for 2 minutes. Turn the scallops, re-cover, and simmer for about 2 minutes longer, until the scallops are opaque all the way through.

3. Sprinkle the chives over the scallops and serve immediately.

Per serving: 4 grams carbohydrates, 28 grams protein, 6 grams fat

Zone Tip

If you want to lose weight for a special event or vacation, your best approach is to exercise more, measure your portions, and choose the "most favorable" foods to eat the closer you get to the date. It's unrealistic and unnecessary to demand this behavior of yourself all the time and much more sensible to make changes that fit into your lifestyle so that success will be yours.

Pan-Seared Asian Scallops

Most recipes for scallops are easy, and this is no exception. I love making these scallops with blood orange juice. Its bright red color is wonderfully startling, and it's pleasingly sweet. If it's not the season for blood oranges, which is December through March, squeeze another type of orange, but don't miss this recipe!

Serves 4

1 tablespoon hoisin sauce
Juice of 1 blood orange
Juice of 1 lemon
1 teaspoon finely chopped lemon zest
1½ pounds scallops
2 teaspoons olive oil
2 garlic cloves, chopped
2 scallions, white and green parts, chopped, or ¼ cup chopped red
    onion
1 tablespoon sesame seeds

1. In a nonreactive bowl, mix together the hoisin sauce, orange juice, lemon juice, and lemon zest. Add the scallops, toss gently to coat, cover, and refrigerate for 1 hour to marinate.

2. In a nonstick skillet, heat the olive oil over medium-high heat. Add the garlic and scallions, and sauté for about 5 minutes, until transparent.

3. Lift the scallops from the marinade, letting the liquid drip back into the bowl, and add them to the skillet. Reserve the marinade.

4. Cook the scallops for 2 to 3 minutes on each side, or until opaque all the way through. Sprinkle the scallops with sesame seeds and remove them from the skillet.

5. Add the reserved marinade to the pan and simmer for about 5 minutes, until the liquids are reduced to about 3 to 4 tablespoons. Pour the sauce over the scallops and serve immediately.

Per serving: 9 grams carbohydrates, 28 grams protein, 4 grams fat

---

Zone Tip

Fermented foods such as miso and yogurt contain beneficial bacteria that help your body break down food, reducing your chances of gastrointestinal upsets. To reap these benefits, check for "live and active cultures" listed on the label, and never boil miso, or it will lose the helpful properties.

Bay Scallops with Sorrel

This is a surprising combination that works really well. Sorrel, a favorable carbohydrate, is an early-spring herb with bright green, heart-shape leaves and a pleasant, slightly acidic flavor. Matching it with wasabi, the hot Japanese horseradish, and dainty bay scallops creates a dish with Asian accents. Serve this with stir-fried vegetables and a fruit crisp for dessert.

Serves 6

Dressing
2½ tablespoons low-sodium tamari
2¼ tablespoons mirin
2 teaspoons toasted sesame oil
1 tablespoon dry sherry
1 tablespoon fresh lemon juice
½ teaspoon wasabi powder
½ tablespoon finely chopped or crushed garlic
½ tablespoon grated fresh ginger

Scallops
4 ounces fresh sorrel or arugula, tough stems removed
2 teaspoons olive oil
1 teaspoon crushed garlic
1 teaspoon grated fresh ginger
2¼ pounds bay or sea scallops (if using sea scallops, cut them in half)
1 tablespoon sesame seeds
Chopped fresh cilantro, for garnish

1. To make the dressing, in a saucepan, stir together the tamari, mirin, sesame oil, sherry, lemon juice, wasabi powder, garlic, and ginger. Bring the contents to a boil over medium-high heat and cook for about 1 minute. Remove the dressing from the heat and set it aside to cool.

2. To prepare the scallops, spread the sorrel on a serving platter. Spoon about ½ cup of the dressing over the sorrel, and toss to mix.

3. Heat a wok over high heat, add the olive oil, and when the oil is hot, reduce the heat to medium. Add the garlic and ginger, and cook, stirring, for about 30 seconds, until the mixture is fragrant but not colored.

4. Add the scallops and stir-fry for about 3 minutes, until they are firm and opaque.

5. Spoon the scallops over the sorrel. Drizzle with enough of the remaining dressing to moisten the sorrel. Sprinkle with sesame seeds and cilantro, and serve.

Per serving: 6 grams carbohydrates, 28 grams protein, 3 grams fat

Scallops with Orange and Sesame Oil

Sea scallops, which are easy to find in most stores that sell fresh fish, should have a pinkish tinge or look creamy white. Any that are bright white and shiny may have been soaked in a preserving solution, which, while not harmful, is absorbed by the scallops and dilutes their flavor. I love how the flavor of orange juice blends with the scallops and red onion. If the scallops are especially large, I suggest you halve or quarter them before threading them on the skewers. If you want, drizzle a little extra sesame oil over the scallops just before you serve them. Serve this with String Beans with Sesame Seeds, page 224, a salad, and the Chocolate-Covered Strawberries on page 263.

Serves 2 as a main course, 4 as an appetizer

¾ pound sea scallops
1 cup orange juice
1 tablespoon toasted sesame oil
5 to 6 scallions (1 bunch), white and green parts, sliced lengthwise
    and diced
1 red onion, quartered, or cut to be same size as the scallops

1. Rinse the scallops and pat them dry. Cut any large ones in half (but they must be large enough for the skewers). Put them in a nonreactive bowl, and add the orange juice, 2 teaspoons of the sesame oil, scallions, and onion. Cover and refrigerate for 1 hour.

2. Preheat the broiler. Soak eight 6-inch wooden skewers in cold water. This keeps them from burning in the broiler.

3. Drain the scallops, reserving the onion. Reserve the marinade. Put the onion in a microwave-safe dish and microwave at High for 1 minute, or until slightly softened.

4. Using 2 skewers for each serving, thread each pair of skewers with scallops and an onion quarter. Lay the skewers on a broiling pan.

5. Broil about 2 inches from the heat source for about 2 minutes, turning the skewers once, until the scallops are cooked through and opaque.

6. In a small saucepan, bring the reserved marinade to a boil, and simmer briskly for about 5 minutes.

7. Drizzle the remaining 1 teaspoon of sesame oil and marinade over the scallops, and serve.

Per main course serving: 5 grams carbohydrates, 28 grams protein, 9 grams fat

---

Zone Tip

If you line up two skewers side by side and spear the fish, meat, vegetables, or fruit with both, the food won't turn and slip during grilling or broiling. This makes the skewers easy to turn and cuts down on frustration.

Steamed Mussels

Mussels are great, and too few home cooks think of preparing them, which is a shame because they are low in fat and low in price! The best way to cook them is to steam them, which takes only minutes. They are ready when the shells open. The most time-consuming part is cleaning the mussels. They can be pretty gritty, and so even though a lot of stores sell very clean mussels, I still recommend soaking them at least once—and twice if they are sandy. Serve this with a warm goat cheese salad. The broth is so delicious with these that you might want to indulge in a piece of whole-grain sourdough or Italian bread to sop it up!

Serves 4

4 pounds mussels, cleaned (approximately 1 pound per person will
   yield about 4 ounces of mussel meat)
Large pinch of baking soda
2 teaspoons olive oil
1 large yellow onion, chopped
3 to 4 garlic cloves, chopped
1 cup dry vermouth or dry white wine, or 12 ounces beer
10 drops hot red pepper sauce
Handful of chopped flat-leaf parsley
2 large tomatoes, diced

1. Put the mussels in a large bowl or pot and add enough cold water to cover by about 2 inches. Add the baking soda, swish to mix, and set aside to soak for 30 minutes. Drain and rinse. If the mussels are still gritty, soak and rinse again. Drain in a colander.

2. Using a stiff-bristle brush, scrub the mussels under cool running water. Make sure to remove any of the bristly beard.

3. In a large stockpot, heat the olive oil over medium-high heat. Add the onion and cook for 2 minutes, until it begins to soften. Add the garlic and cook 1 minute longer, or until softened but not colored.

4. Add the vermouth and bring the contents to a boil. Stir in the hot sauce and parsley, and then add the mussels. Lower the heat so that the liquid simmers, cover the pan, and cook for 8 to 10 minutes, adjusting the heat to maintain the simmer, until the mussels open. Discard any mussels that do not open.

5. Add the tomatoes and stir to mix. Spoon the mussels into shallow soup bowls and ladle broth over them.

Per serving: 10 grams carbohydrates, 27 grams protein, 2 grams fat

Mussels with Artichoke Hearts

As anyone knows who has read other chapters in this book, I am extremely fond of artichoke hearts and always have a few cans or frozen packages at the ready. Here, I use artichoke hearts that are packed in brine—never those "fancy" ones that are packed in oil and herbs. Be sure to soak the mussels at least once, despite how clean they appear at the market, to rid them of any sand or grit. You'll be crazy about the broth for these mussels. Serve this up in shallow bowls with a salad, some roasted vegetables, and a piece of whole-grain bread. It's nice to end this meal with grilled fruit kabobs, but if you do, forget the bread!

Serves 4

About 4 pounds mussels, cleaned
Large pinch of baking soda
2 teaspoons olive oil
1 large sweet onion, such as Vidalia or Maui, chopped
3 to 4 garlic cloves, chopped
4 cups dry vermouth
2 tomatoes, diced
1 15-ounce can artichoke hearts, drained, rinsed, and quartered

1. Put the mussels in a large bowl or pot and add enough cold water to cover by about 2 inches. Add the baking soda, swish to mix, and set aside to soak for 30 minutes. (The baking soda helps remove the sand from the mussels.) Drain, rinse, return to the bowl, and cover again with cold water (no baking soda this time). Set aside to soak for 30 minutes longer. If the mussels are very gritty, soak and rinse a third time. Drain in a colander.

2. In a stockpot, heat the olive oil over medium heat. Add the onion and sauté for about 5 minutes, until softened. Add the garlic and sauté about 1 minute longer, until softened but not colored.

3. Add 2 cups of the vermouth, bring the contents to a boil over medium-high heat, and cook rapidly for 7 minutes, or until reduced by half.

4. Add the remaining 2 cups of vermouth, the tomatoes, and the drained mussels. Bring the contents to a simmer, cover, and simmer for about 5 minutes. Add the artichoke hearts and stir the mixture well from bottom to top. Re-cover and cook 2 to 3 minutes longer, or until the mussels open. Discard any that do not open.

5. Spoon the mussels, tomatoes, and artichoke hearts into shallow soup bowls and ladle broth over them.

Per serving: 17 grams carbohydrates, 27 grams protein, 2 grams fat

Salmon Salad

I wasn't certain if this recipe belonged in this chapter or in Chapter 4 with the appetizers and salads. In the end I decided it was so rich and satisfying that it deserved main-course status. I suggest using leftover salmon or char, but this is so good that it's worth cooking fish just for the occasion. You can double, triple, or quadruple the ingredients for more servings. The guacamole binds the fish, much as mayonnaise does, but tastes so much better! Whenever possible, I use wild Pacific salmon. It has fewer toxins than other salmon and more omega-3 fatty acids.

Serves 1

4 ounces leftover salmon or arctic char
¼ cup Guacamole, page 66
¼ cup canned and drained kidney beans

1 rib celery, diced
1 tablespoon chopped red or white onion
1 teaspoon chopped fresh cilantro
Hot red pepper sauce
Herbamare
2 cups torn lettuce or mixed greens
½ cup white or red seedless grapes
1 ripe pear, sliced

1. In a mixing bowl, flake the salmon into small pieces with a fork. Add the guacamole, kidney beans, celery, onion, and cilantro. Toss, and season to taste with hot sauce and Herbamare.

2. Put the lettuce greens on a serving plate and top with the salmon mixture. Arrange the grapes and pear slices on the plate, and serve.

Per serving: 36 grams carbohydrates, 28 grams protein, 12 grams fat

Zone Tip

Take at least four omega-3 fish oil capsules (1 gram) every day. (Take them before meals so that you don't taste fish oil in your mouth.) Fish oil is great for mental alertness. There's a good reason fish is called brain food! The benefits of these fatty acids are by now nearly legendary. Teamed with a Zone-favorable diet, they help prevent heart disease, some cancers, diabetes, rheumatoid arthritis, and more. Look for pharmaceutical-grade fish oil for purity.

Salmon with Orange and Miso Sauce

Salmon, which is a meaty, firm fish, can stand up to a slightly sweet marinade such as this one made with yellow miso, mirin (sweet rice wine), and Splenda. I enjoy making this in the late afternoon and savoring it while it marinates. I garnish it with scallions and cilantro to play out the Asian theme. Try it along with olive oil-drizzled asparagus or summer squash. To make this a Zone-favorable meal, add a bowl of Lentil Soup on page 67.

Serves 4

⅓ cup yellow miso*
2 tablespoons orange juice
1 tablespoon mirin
1 tablespoon shredded or chopped fresh ginger
2 teaspoons low-sodium soy sauce
1 teaspoon grated orange zest
1 teaspoon Splenda
1½ pounds salmon fillets with skin, cut into 4 pieces
4 scallions, white and green parts, thinly sliced diagonally
2 tablespoons chopped fresh cilantro

1. In a nonreactive bowl, mix together the miso, orange juice, mirin, ginger, soy sauce, orange zest, and Splenda.

2. Lay the salmon in a shallow glass dish and pour the marinade over the fish. Turn to coat. Cover and refrigerate for at least 1 hour and up to 3 hours.

3. Preheat the broiler.

4. Lay the salmon, skin-side down, on the broiling pan and broil for about 4 minutes, until a glaze forms on the surface. Cover loosely with foil and broil about 4 minutes longer, until cooked through. The time will depend on the thickness of the fish.

5. Serve garnished with scallions and cilantro.

Per serving: 5 grams carbohydrates, 28 grams protein, 2 grams fat

*Yellow miso is made from fermented soybeans and rice and has the mildest flavor of all miso, which is why it's sometimes called "sweet miso." Miso is used in many Japanese recipes and is easy to find in Asian markets.

Zone Tip

Always try to make more food than you need, so that you can have leftovers. Sometimes I'll freeze an extra pound of an oily fish such as salmon or bluefish, which I prefer for their omega-3 fatty acids. I just seal individual portions in plastic wrap and slip them inside a plastic zip bag. I remove the fish from the freezer the night before (or in the morning before work) and let it thaw in the refrigerator. This way, I simply heat it, unwrapped, in the microwave for a minute or two and have a great meal! It's best to use it within a month.

Salmon with Hot-and-Sweet Mustard Sauce

Once you taste this mustard sauce, you may want to double or triple the recipe and keep some in the refrigerator for up to 2 months to

use not only for salmon but also for other red-meat fish such as red rainbow trout and arctic char. It's also yummy on chicken breasts. You'll be able to have a delicious dinner on the table in minutes! I like the salmon with string beans, a salad, and Almond Biscotti, page 252, for dessert.

Serves 4

2 tablespoons grainy Dijon mustard
1 tablespoon low-sodium tamari or soy sauce
1 tablespoon mirin
2 teaspoons brown rice syrup or honey
1 teaspoon crushed garlic
1 teaspoon finely shredded fresh ginger
1 scallion, white and green parts, sliced diagonally
1 to 2 dashes hot red pepper sauce
2 tablespoons chopped fresh cilantro
1½ pounds salmon steaks, cut 1½ inches thick

1. Preheat the broiler, or prepare a charcoal or gas grill so that the coals or heating elements are medium-hot.

2. In a small bowl, stir together the mustard, tamari, mirin, brown rice syrup, garlic, ginger, scallion, and hot sauce to taste. Stir in the cilantro.

3. Spread the mixture on one side of the fish and arrange them, sauce-side up, on a broiling tray, or lay them on a lightly oiled grill grate. Broil or grill for about 5 minutes. Turn the fish and cook 5 minutes longer, or until reddish pink opaque in the center. Cut into 4 equal portions.

Per serving: 5 grams carbohydrates, 28 grams protein, 0 grams fat

Zone Tip
Want to know another benefit of omega-3 fats? They soften your skin!

Baked New England Cod

Living as I do in New England, I'm partial to cod, which is a mild-tasting whitefish that is low fat. Other fish such as hake, whiting, or haddock would work just as well in this recipe, and all are equally low in fat and mild. In the old days, New England fishermen called all white-fleshed fish cod or scrod, and so you might see old recipes for scrod and wonder what it is. Once you have the ingredients ready, this one takes about 5 minutes to prepare and then a mere 20 minutes to cook. Serve with half a small sweet potato, steamed broccoli or asparagus, and a salad.

Serves 4

1 tablespoon olive oil
Juice of 1 lemon
1 garlic clove, crushed
2 tablespoons snipped fresh dill and/or chopped flat-leaf parsley
Herbamare
Paprika
Lemon-pepper seasoning
1½ pounds cod fillets
2 tablespoons whole wheat bread crumbs

1. Preheat the oven to 350°F.

2. In a shallow, glass baking dish, mix together the olive oil, lemon juice, garlic, and dill. Season to taste with Herbamare, paprika, and lemon-pepper seasoning.

3. Lay the fillets in the dish and turn to coat. Sprinkle the bread crumbs over the fish as evenly as possible.

4. Bake for 20 minutes, until the fish is opaque and flakes easily.

Per serving: 6 grams carbohydrates, 28 grams protein, 3.5 grams fat

Zone Tip

More fish spoils at home than anywhere else. Standard refrigerators are not cold enough to store fish, which keeps almost twice as well at 32 to 33 degrees (the temperature when it's buried in ice) as it does at 40 degrees, the temperature of most refrigerators. To solve this problem, fill the vegetable bin or a baking pan with ice (or ice packs, which are less messy) and do your best to bury your wrapped fish in there; you will maintain the quality of your fish for a lot longer. Still, it's always a good idea to eat fish within twenty-four hours of purchase.

Seared Tuna with Arugula Salad

The key to this great meal is really, really fresh, high-quality tuna. I try to buy what they call sushi-quality tuna, which means it is absolutely fine to eat raw! I cook it just a little so that it is rare, juicy, tender, and meaty. If you overcook tuna, it quickly becomes dry and not the way I like it. But it's up to you! If your market does not carry sushi-quality tuna, go for grade 2/B, and make sure the tuna is fresh on the day you buy it. Plan to cook it the same day. I like to accompany tuna with a little wasabi, which is Japanese horseradish and lends great heat to the dish. To round out this meal so that it's in the Zone, include a quarter cup of black beans with every serving, a salad, and fresh fruit for dessert.

Serves 2

Tuna
2 tablespoons sesame seeds
1 tablespoon poppy seeds
1 tablespoon dried onion flakes
1 tablespoon garlic powder

Coarse salt and freshly ground pepper
2 4-ounce sushi-quality tuna steaks, such as yellowfin, about ¾ inch
   thick
1 tablespoon olive oil

Arugula salad
2 tablespoons fresh lemon juice
1 tablespoon olive oil
Coarse salt and freshly ground pepper
4 cups stemmed arugula leaves or baby spinach
2 cups thinly sliced fennel (about 1 small bulb)
1 cup plain artichoke hearts, quartered*

1. To make the tuna, in a small bowl, stir together the sesame seeds,
poppy seeds, onion flakes, and garlic powder. Add about ¼ teaspoon
salt and ¾ teaspoon pepper, and mix well.

2. Spread the seasoning mixture on a large sheet of wax paper. Press
the tuna steaks into the mixture and turn to coat both sides. Pat the
seasoning into the steaks.

3. In a nonstick skillet, heat the tablespoon of olive oil over medium
heat. Add the tuna steaks and cook for 2 minutes on each side for
rare, or until cooked to the desired degree of doneness.

4. To make the salad, in a large bowl, whisk together the lemon
juice and tablespoon of olive oil. Season with about ¼ teaspoon salt
and ¾ teaspoon pepper, and whisk again. Add the arugula, fennel,
and artichoke hearts, and toss well.

5. Divide the salad between two plates and top each with a tuna
steak. Serve immediately.

Per serving: 21 grams carbohydrates, 28 grams protein, 7 grams fat

*Be sure to use frozen artichoke hearts or those canned in brine. In other words, do not use artichoke hearts marinated in oil and vinegar and spices.

Grilled Tuna Salad

This may not meet your expectations of tuna salad—I predict it will far exceed them! The tuna is grilled and then served with grilled vegetables on a bed of mesclun. Very elegant! If you don't happen to like tuna as much as I do, you could use any firm, oily fish such as swordfish, salmon, arctic char, striped bass, or bluefish. You can also vary the vegetables to customize the salad to your liking. Serve with grilled fruit kabobs.

Serves 4

Tuna
¼ cup dry vermouth
2 tablespoons olive oil
2 tablespoons fresh lemon juice
2 garlic cloves, crushed
1 tablespoon grainy mustard
½ teaspoon wasabi powder
Fresh thyme and rosemary, chopped
Herbamare
1 pound fresh tuna, salmon, or swordfish steak, or similar full-
    flavored fish such as artic char, striped bass, or bluefish, ¾ to
    1 inch thick

Vegetables
¾ cup olive oil
¼ cup balsamic vinegar

2 garlic cloves, chopped
Sea salt and freshly ground pepper
Herbamare
3 red, yellow, or orange bell peppers, sliced into wide strips
2 red onions, halved
Vegetable oil cooking spray
2 cups mesclun mix or other mixed small salad greens

1. To make the tuna, in a shallow, nonreactive dish, mix together the vermouth, olive oil, lemon juice, garlic, mustard, wasabi powder, thyme, rosemary, and Herbamare to taste.

2. Add the tuna and turn several times to coat. Cover and refrigerate for at least 30 minutes and up to 2 hours.

3. To make the vegetables, in a large bowl, mix together the olive oil, vinegar, garlic, and salt, black pepper, and Herbamare to taste. Add the bell peppers and onion halves. Set aside at room temperature to marinate for the same length of time as the fish.

4. Prepare a charcoal or gas grill. Lightly coat the grill rack with vegetable oil cooking spray. The coals or heating elements are ready when they are medium-hot.

5. Lift the vegetables, letting most of the liquid drip back into the bowl. Grill for 5 to 8 minutes, or until softened and lightly charred.

6. After the vegetables have been on the grill for 2 to 3 minutes, lift the fish from the marinade, again letting most of the liquid drip back into the dish. On the grill rack or in a grilling basket, grill the tuna for 2½ minutes each side so that it is rare. If using other fish, cook for about 4 to 5 minutes each side, or until opaque in the center.

7. Pile the mesclun on each of four serving plates. Lay the fish on top of the greens, and then top with grilled vegetables.

Per serving: 8 grams carbohydrates, 28 grams protein, 5.5 grams fat

Red Snapper Fillets Steamed over a Bed of Fennel

Red snapper is one of my favorites. The white, firm, meaty fish is caught in the mid-Atlantic Ocean, the Caribbean, and the Gulf of Mexico. On the West Coast, they label red rockfish as Pacific red snapper, but it doesn't taste too much like real snapper. Most fish recipes are wonderfully versatile, because many different types of fish can be used with them. For example, here, you can substitute grouper, tilefish, or striped bass. This recipe has no added fat (the fish is essentially fat free), and so you will have to get your fat in another part of the meal. Try it with the Arugula and Kidney Bean Salad on page 82 and fruit for dessert. And don't worry about the wine—the alcohol cooks off.

Serves 2

1 fennel bulb
1 carrot, cut into matchsticks
1 cup dry white wine or dry vermouth
Sea salt and freshly ground pepper
8 ounces red snapper fillets, skinned
4 lemon wedges

1. Trim the fennel fronds from the bulb, reserving the bulb, and chop enough of the fronds to measure 2 good tablespoons. Set aside for garnish, and discard the rest of the fronds or save them for another use.

2. Trim the stalks from the fennel bulb, cut away any discolorations, quarter the bulb lengthwise, and then slice it thinly crosswise.

3. In a skillet large enough to hold the fillets (halve them if necessary), combine the sliced fennel, carrot, and ½ cup of the wine.

Cook, covered, over medium-low heat for 10 to 15 minutes, or until the fennel is slightly wilted and beginning to stick to the pan. Add the remaining ½ cup of wine to the pan, and season with salt and pepper.

4. Sprinkle the fillets with salt and pepper, and lay them on top of the vegetables. Cover the pan and steam the fish over medium-low heat for 10 to 15 minutes, or until the flesh is opaque all the way through.

5. Transfer the fish and vegetables to a serving platter. Serve garnished with lemon wedges and the fennel greens.

Per serving: 15 grams carbohydrates, 24 grams protein, 0 grams fat

Zone Tip

Most Zone users are aware of the heart-health benefits of omega-3 fish oils. Less well-known is that omega-3 fatty acids also help combat Crohn's disease, ulcerative colitis, and lupus, as well as decreasing the need for anti-inflammatory drugs.

Poached Snapper alla Livornese

Poached fish is always moist and tender. The gentle method is kind to nearly any type of fish, whether it's filleted, cut into steaks, or left whole. Barely cover the fish with the poaching liquid, and cook gently. The shallots, which are sautéed briefly to heighten their flavor before the fish is added to the pan, provide subtle depth. Once you get in the habit of cooking with shallots, you will be hooked. They are small onions that resemble a large clove of garlic covered with coppery, papery skin and which have a mild flavor that some say tastes slightly of garlic. I make this with tomatoes, similar to dishes made in Livorno, Italy, but you could replace them with mushrooms and add a little dill or another herb. All good! I serve this with Whipped Cauliflower, page 241, a salad, and a cup of sliced strawberries for dessert.

Serves 6

2 pounds red snapper, lemon sole, striped bass, or halibut fillets
4 shallots
¼ cup dry white wine or water
3 tablespoons drained capers
1 pound ripe plum tomatoes, chopped, or 2 cups canned, drained and chopped
4 sprigs flat-leaf parsley, chopped
Sea salt and freshly ground pepper

1. Cut the fish into six equal portions, rinse, and pat them dry.

2. In a large nonstick pan, sauté the shallots over medium heat for 3 to 4 minutes, or until translucent. Add a little water to the pan to prevent the shallots from sticking.

3. Lay the fish in the pan in a single layer. Add the wine and capers, and cook for about 2 minutes, until heated through. Add a little extra water, if needed, to cover the fish. Add the tomatoes and parsley, and season to taste with salt and pepper.

4. Cover the pan and poach the fish for 6 to 10 minutes. After 6 minutes, check with a fork, and cook only until tender and opaque. Do not overcook.

5. Lift the fish from the pan. Check the pan sauce for seasonings, and adjust as needed. Spoon the sauce over the fish and serve.

Per serving: 8 grams carbohydrates, 28 grams protein, 0 grams fat

Roasted Red Snapper with Fennel

Served alongside Steamed Butternut Squash with Bok Choy and Mushrooms on page 236, or a similar vegetable, this dish makes an outstanding Zone-friendly meal. I often pair fennel with fish because the combo is so darn tasty and because fennel is easy to find (it looks like an overgrown, lopsided celery root with wispy fronds). The latter point isn't true for everything in this recipe, however. The pumpkin oil was a discovery I made while strolling down the aisle of Whole Foods Market one day. It has an appealingly pungent aroma and distinctive flavor that, to me, tastes "like autumn." If you can't find it, substitute toasted sesame oil, flaxseed oil, or olive oil. I love Spicy Herbamare—which is sold next to Herbamare in health food stores—for its extra kick here, but you can use chili powder or Emeril's Southwest Seasoning, if you prefer. Finally, for the whole snapper, which is a wonderful fish, feel free to substitute sea bass or another whole, mild, white-fleshed fish.

Serves 4

Olive oil cooking spray
2 fennel bulbs, fronds trimmed
2 1-pound whole snappers with head and tail attached
1 garlic clove, pressed
Spicy Herbamare or sea salt and freshly ground pepper
1 tablespoon pumpkin seed oil or another nut oil, such as walnut or
   almond
¼ cup dry white wine

1. Preheat the oven to 450°F. Line a pan large enough to hold the fish with aluminum foil, and coat the foil lightly with olive oil cooking spray.

2. Core the fennel bulbs and slice them into rings about 1 inch thick.

3. Cut three or four crosswise slashes, about 1 inch long and ¼ inch deep, in each side of both fish so that the seasonings and heat can permeate the meat. Season both fish inside and out with the garlic and Herbamare. Scatter the fennel around the fish and season with Herbamare. Pour the pumpkin seed oil over the fish and the fennel.

4. Roast the fish for 20 minutes and then add the wine to the pan. It will evaporate during cooking. Continue cooking 30 to 40 minutes longer, or until cooked through. Peek into the slashes to see if the fish is white all the way to the bone.

5. Cut off and discard the heads. Using two spatulas, lift the fish from the pan and transfer it to a platter. Cut down the backbone and lift the top of the spine from the fish. Work carefully so that all the small bones come out with the backbone.

6. Serve the fish with the fennel on top.

Per serving: 9 grams carbohydrates, 28 grams protein, 4 grams fat

Roasted Red Snapper with Vegetables

Squash slices, diced tomato, mushrooms, and herbs mingle with the fish to form a heady sauce that's a hands-down winner. I like to use a whole fish that weighs about 1¾ pounds, such as red snapper, but fillets can fill the bill. I urge you to try a whole fish, though. Nothing is more moist or succulent, and your fish merchant will make sure the fish is well cleaned with the gills removed. Filleting is easy once the fish is cooked. To complete this meal, serve a side of greens, a glass of chilled white wine, and a cantaloupe quarter for dessert.

Serves 4

Olive oil cooking spray
1 1¾-pound whole red snapper or other large fish, such as sea bass
Coarse sea salt and freshly ground pepper
4 garlic cloves, finely minced
1 tablespoon chopped flat-leaf parsley
1 tablespoon snipped fresh dill
1 large ripe tomato, diced
3 zucchini, cut into ¾-inch-thick rounds
3 summer squashes, cut into ¾-inch-thick rounds
1 yellow onion, diced
¾ pound white mushrooms, stemmed and halved
1 tablespoon olive oil
Herbamare

1. Preheat oven to 475°F. Coat a roasting pan large enough to hold the fish with olive oil cooking spray.

2. Wash the fish inside and out, and pat dry with a paper towel. Sprinkle salt and pepper in the cavity.

3. In a small bowl, mix together the garlic, parsley, and dill. Rub the mixture over the fish, inside and out. Lay the fish in the roasting pan.

4. Spread the tomato over the fish. Arrange the zucchini, squash, onion, and mushrooms around the fish, and drizzle with olive oil. Season to taste with Herbamare and pepper.

5. Roast for 30 to 45 minutes, depending on the thickness, until the fish is cooked through and opaque in the center.

6. Cut off and discard the head, if necessary. Using two spatulas, transfer the fish to a platter. Cut along the backbone and lift the top

of the spine from the meat. Work carefully so that all the small bones come out with the backbone.

7. Transfer the vegetables and juices to a bowl, and serve alongside the fish.

Per serving: 6 grams carbohydrates, 24 grams protein, 3 grams fat

---

Zone Tip
A smart kitchen has a half-sheet baking pan (12″ ×17″) and a good, heavy roasting pan with sturdy handles. Buy heavy-gauge weights that resist warping.

Grilled Swordfish in Lime-Cilantro Sauce

Swordfish takes beautifully to marinades, and this one is among the easiest and tastiest I know. People often ask me how marinades can be "in the Zone," because they are hard to quantify and usually contain oil. I explain that when they are quite liquidy, as mine tend to be, they are not counted—because they slide off the food. In dishes in which some of the marinade sticks to the food during cooking, I halve the nutritional counts for the marinade ingredients (reflected in each recipe). In this recipe, the fish should not be marinated for longer than an hour or so, because the acid from the vermouth and lime juice breaks the protein down fairly quickly. An hour is plenty of time for this process to occur, and even a half hour is long enough for the swordfish to pick up the desired flavor.

Serves 4

¼ cup dry vermouth or dry white wine
Juice of 1 lime
1 tablespoon extra-virgin olive oil
1 tablespoon low-sodium tamari* or soy sauce
1 tablespoon fresh chopped cilantro
1½ pounds swordfish or Chilean sea bass steaks, rinsed in cold water
Olive oil cooking spray

1. In a gallon-size sealable plastic bag or 9″ × 12″ glass dish, mix
together the vermouth, lime juice, olive oil, tamari, and cilantro. Add
the swordfish. If using a plastic bag, squeeze out the air, seal the
bag, and turn it to coat the fish. If using a dish, turn the fish to coat,
and cover the dish with plastic wrap.

2. Refrigerate for 1 hour, or marinate at room temperature for 30
minutes.

3. Coat the broiler pan or rack with olive oil cooking spray and
adjust it so that it's about 5 inches from the heat source. Preheat the
broiler.

4. Transfer the fish to the broiler pan, reserving the marinade. Broil
for about 4 minutes on each side, or until it flakes easily with a fork.

5. Meanwhile, in a small saucepan, bring the marinade to a boil over
medium-high heat, reduce the heat slightly, and simmer briskly for 5
minutes.

6. Serve the swordfish with the sauce poured over it.

Per serving: 0 grams carbohydrates, 28 grams protein, 3.5 grams fat

*Tamari is a naturally fermented, aged, low-sodium soy product
made without additives or preservatives. It's wheat free, while soy
sauce (also called shoyu) includes wheat. Tamari is prized by those
with wheat allergies.

Striped Bass in Parchment Paper with Vegetables

Believe it or not, the most crucial ingredient for success with this recipe is the parchment paper. It's packaged like wax paper and sold with the other baking and storage products in most supermarkets. At one time, it was a staple in all kitchens. Nowadays it's primarily bakers who use parchment paper, but I think every home cook should have a roll too, since it makes for a gorgeous way to cook delicate dishes such as this one. If striped bass isn't available, use grouper, cod, or haddock—although I suggest you stay clear of very thin fish such as sole. Try this with the vegetables I recommend here, or substitute spinach, Swiss chard, mushrooms, fennel, bok choy, or pea pods. The vegetable slices should be of uniform thickness; it's a good idea to use a vegetable peeler to get the carrots nice and thin. If the fish you use is very mild, up the seasonings a little. And take care when you unwrap the parchment paper, because the steam is hot! Serve this with wild rice and fresh fruit.

Serves 4

1½ pounds striped bass fillets
1 garlic clove, crushed
Fresh snipped dill or chopped cilantro
Herbamare and freshly ground pepper
4 zucchini, thinly sliced
4 summer squashes, thinly sliced
2 carrots, thinly sliced

1. Preheat the oven to 350°F.

2. Center the fish on a large sheet of parchment paper (about 40 inches) on a baking sheet. Sprinkle the garlic over the fish, and

season to taste with dill, Herbamare, and pepper. Put half of the zucchini, squash, and carrot slices on top of the fish, and season with more dill, Herbamare, and pepper. Distribute the rest of the vegetables on the sides of the fish.

3. Fold the parchment paper around the fish and vegetables so that one end is open, similar to a paper bag. This will allow the steam to vent.

4. Bake for 15 to 20 minutes, depending on the thickness of the fish, until it's cooked through and the vegetables are tender. Unwrap very carefully and transfer the fish and vegetables to a serving platter.

Per serving: 6 grams carbohydrates, 28 grams protein, 0 grams fat

Striped Bass with Red Peppers and Portobello Mushrooms

If you see striped bass in the market, buy it. The firm, white-fleshed fish is sublime. It's mild tasting, and yet with the first bite you know you are eating a superior fish. In New England, where I live, fresh wild striped bass is available for only a few months in the spring and summer, and I look forward to it all the rest of the year. Ask the fish merchant to remove the skin for you. I have made this recipe with halibut, which tastes very good, too. Serve with a salad and Apple Crisp on page 257.

Serves 4

2 teaspoons olive oil
4 garlic cloves, crushed
1½ pounds striped bass
Herbamare
Emeril's Southwest Seasoning or another spicy seasoning
4 portobello mushrooms, sliced into 16 pieces
1 red bell pepper, sliced into strips
6 pitted kalamata olives, roughly chopped
2 tablespoons snipped fresh dill
2 tablespoons chopped flat-leaf parsley
Splash of aged balsamic vinegar

1. Preheat the oven to 350°F.

2. In a nonstick frying pan, heat the olive oil over medium heat. Add the garlic and sauté for about 1 minute, until softened but not colored. Add the fish, season with Herbamare and Southwest Seasoning, and cook for about 3 minutes on each side, until just seared or lightly browned.

3. Transfer the fish to a shallow casserole large enough to hold it in a single layer. Set aside.

4. Add the mushrooms and bell pepper to the frying pan, and cook over medium heat for 4 to 5 minutes, or until softened. Add the olives, dill, parsley, and vinegar. Mix gently and taste for seasoning.

5. Spoon the vegetables over the fish, and bake for about 20 minutes, until the fish is cooked through and opaque in the center. Serve immediately.

Per serving: 3 grams carbohydrates, 28 grams protein, 4.5 grams fat

Haddock with Artichoke Hearts

Once again, I turn to canned or frozen artichoke hearts to dress up mild haddock. Add a tomato, a good amount of garlic, and some bright-tasting lemon juice, and the dish is absolutely tantalizing. I like this with a little brown rice (about ⅕ cup per serving) and an assortment of stir-fried vegetables such as carrots, zucchini, and summer squash.

Serves 4

2 teaspoons olive oil
2 garlic cloves, crushed
1½ pounds haddock fillets, cut into 4 pieces
Sea salt and freshly ground pepper
Herbamare
9 ounces frozen or canned and drained artichoke hearts, quartered
1 tomato, diced
Juice of 1 lemon

1. In a large nonstick skillet, heat the olive oil over medium-high heat. Add the garlic and sauté for about 1 minute, until softened but not colored.

2. Season the haddock lightly with salt, pepper, and Herbamare, and lay it in the skillet. Cook for 4 minutes, turn, and cook 3 to 4 minutes longer, or until nearly cooked through.

3. Add the artichoke hearts and tomato, and cook about 3 minutes longer, until the fish is opaque in the center.

4. Transfer the fish to a platter. Add the lemon juice to the pan, stir, and cook for about 1 minute, until the sauce reduces slightly. Pour the pan sauce over the fish and serve.

Per serving: 6 grams carbohydrates, 28 grams protein, 3.5 grams fat

Tilapia with Salsa

Tilapia, also known as Saint Peter's fish, has been successfully farm-raised for years around the world. U.S. aquaculturists grow it in indoor ponds, and in recent years it has become one of our most popular fish. The mild, white flesh is universally appealing and makes tilapia just the ticket for serving with bold flavors such as this jazzy salsa. This preparation tastes great with a green salad, some steamed asparagus, and Chocolate-Covered Strawberries, page 263, for dessert.

Serves 4

Salsa
2 to 3 tomatoes (about ¾ pound), diced, or 1 14½-ounce can diced
  tomatoes
1 8-ounce can black beans, drained and rinsed
½ cup chopped fresh cilantro
¼ teaspoon red pepper, optional
¼ cup chopped pitted black olives
¼ cup store-bought salsa
½ avocado, diced, optional

Fish
1½ pounds tilapia fillets
Olive oil cooking spray
Ground cumin
Sea salt and freshly ground black pepper

1. To make the salsa, in a mixing bowl, stir together the tomatoes, black beans, cilantro, red pepper (if using), olives, salsa, and avocado (if using). If you're not serving the salsa right away, cover and refrigerate for up to 1 day.

2. To cook the fish, preheat the broiler.

3. Lay the fish in the broiling tray. Lightly coat the fillets with olive oil cooking spray, and season with cumin, salt, and black pepper.

4. Broil for 5 minutes, turning once. (If the fillets are thicker than ¼ to ⅓ inch, they may need a little longer cooking.)

5. Serve the fish with the salsa on the side.

Per serving: 14 grams carbohydrates, 28 grams protein, 6 grams fat

---

Zone Tip
Beans are rich sources of antioxidants. The darker the beans, the more antioxidants they contain. Beans also offer a healthy dose of fiber, calcium, and B vitamins and are a good source of favorable carbohydrates.

Hoisin-Wasabi Sablefish

Sablefish, also called black cod, is a wonderful-tasting, oily saltwater fish that is high in valuable omega-3 oils and in minerals such as iron, zinc, and calcium. It's not always easy to obtain, though, and so I suggest salmon or arctic char as a substitute. The pomegranate balsamic vinegar or pomegranate juice adds a dash of rich, fruity flavor, but because this ingredient also is not so easy to get your hands on, I have made it optional. I serve this with Oven-Roasted Orange Vegetables, page 244, and a salad.

Serves 4

2 tablespoons hoisin sauce
2 tablespoons dry sherry
¾ teaspoon wasabi paste*

1 tablespoon teriyaki sauce
1 teaspoon shredded ginger
½ teaspoon pomegranate balsamic vinegar, or 2 tablespoons pomegranate juice, optional*
1½ pounds sable, salmon, or arctic char fillets, cut into 4 pieces

1. In a small bowl, whisk together the hoisin sauce, sherry, wasabi
paste, teriyaki sauce, ginger, and vinegar, if using.

2. Lay the fish in a shallow glass or other nonreactive dish. Spread
most of the sauce over the fish and set aside to marinate for 20
minutes. If you must leave it for any longer, refrigerate it. (Do not let
the fish marinate longer than 2 hours.)

3. Preheat the broiler.

4. Transfer the fish to a broiling tray, reserving any remains of sauce
in the dish. Broil for 4 minutes, turn, and cook 5 to 6 minutes longer,
or until the fish is cooked through and opaque in the center. The
time depends on the thickness of the fish.

5. Transfer the fish to a serving platter, and top with any remaining
sauce. Serve immediately.

Per serving: 8 grams carbohydrates, 28 grams protein, 0 grams fat

*Wasabi may be sold as a paste and usually in a tube, or in a jar as a
powder that you mix with water to make a paste. It works either
way in this recipe.
   Pomegranate balsamic vinegar is sold in specialty markets, and
pomegranate juice is sold in natural food stores.

Herbed Grouper

When I discovered Emeril's Southwest Essence, I went wild. At the same time, I started using lemon-pepper seasoning and dill seasonings (I like Frontier's Dash of Dill). These spice mixtures don't contain salt and have no fat, protein, or carbohydrates, so you can go a little wild, too! I like them with grouper, but they're also delicious with red snapper, orange roughy, cod, and catfish. Although I say "go wild," it's wise to use a little discretion until you taste how powerful they are. Serve this fish accompanied by Steamed Butternut Squash with Bok Choy and Mushrooms, page 236, to round out the meal and with fruit for dessert.

Serves 2

2 teaspoons olive oil
1 or 2 garlic cloves, crushed
8 ounces grouper, cod, or catfish fillets
Lemon-pepper seasoning
Dill seasoning
Emeril's Southwest Essence or chili powder
Herbamare
Juice of 1 lemon

1. In a medium nonstick skillet, heat the olive oil over medium heat. Add the garlic and sauté for 1 to 2 minutes, until it's softened and fragrant but not colored.

2. Lay the fish in the skillet and sprinkle it with lemon-pepper seasoning, dill seasoning, Southwest Essence, and Herbamare to taste. Sauté for 4 minutes, turn, and cook 4 to 5 minutes longer, or until the fish flakes easily and is opaque all the way through.

3. Add the lemon juice and cook for a few seconds, swirling the skillet to incorporate the lemon juice with the pan juices. Serve immediately with pan juices spooned over the fish.

Per serving: 0 grams carbohydrates, 22 grams protein, 3 grams fat

Grilled Mahimahi with Strawberries

I was astounded the first time I paired mahimahi with strawberries on the grill. I was making dinner and noticed some strawberries in the refrigerator that would not last much longer. So, to avoid having to throw them out, I tried them on the fish and just loved how their sweetness mingled with the spiciness of the chili powder, Herbamare, and garlic. The fish is especially good with guacamole, but if you don't have time to make your own from the recipe on page 66, use the commercial stuff. To expand this into a Zone-friendly meal, add a tossed salad, steamed zucchini, and then blueberry yogurt for dessert.

Serves 4

2 garlic cloves, mashed
2 teaspoons olive oil
1½ pounds mahimahi fillets
Chili powder
Spicy Herbamare
¼ cup chopped cilantro
Olive oil cooking spray
6 strawberries, sliced
3 tablespoons Guacamole, page 66

1. In a small bowl, mix together the garlic and olive oil. Spread the mixture over the fish.

2. Lay the fish on a plate and sprinkle with chili powder, Herbamare, and cilantro. Refrigerate for 30 minutes.

3. Prepare a charcoal or gas grill. Lightly coat the grill grate with olive oil cooking spray. The coals or heating elements are ready when they are medium-hot.

4. Grill the mahimahi skin-side down for 5 minutes. Turn, and lay the strawberries on top of the fish. Grill about 5 minutes longer, until the fish is cooked through and just beginning to turn opaque in the center.

5. Serve with the guacamole on the side.

Per serving: 5 grams carbohydrates, 28 grams protein, 9 grams fat

Fillet of Sole with Grapes and Bananas

Don't be put off by the idea of sole with grapes and bananas. Try it. It's surprisingly delicious and a snap to prepare. The fruit's sweetness offsets the lightly seasoned fish, for a rich and satisfying meal that needs no more than steamed zucchini and a green salad to be a Zone-favorable experience.

Serves 4

4 5-ounce sole fillets
Herbamare

Freshly ground pepper
1 tablespoon olive oil
Juice of 1 lemon
1 banana, thinly sliced
1 cup white or red seedless grapes, halved if large
1 tablespoon finely chopped flat-leaf parsley
1 tablespoon finely snipped fresh dill

1. Lightly season the fillets with Herbamare and pepper.

2. In a large nonstick frying pan, heat the oil over medium heat. Lay
the fillets in the pan and cook, turning once, for about 3 minutes,
until the fish is cooked through and opaque. Transfer the fillets to a
platter and cover loosely with foil to keep warm.

3. Put the banana, grapes, and lemon juice in the pan. Cook over
medium heat for about 2 minutes, tilting and swirling the pan to
ensure even cooking, until the fruit softens, turns golden, and the
liquid evaporates.

4. Pour the contents of the pan over the fillets, and sprinkle with
parsley and dill.

Per serving: 6 grams carbohydrates, 28 grams protein, 3.5 grams fat

Gary's Super Bowl Fish Stew

I named this stew after my friend Gary, who sells fish at the Whole
Foods Market where I shop. He is always ready with a suggestion
and sells only the freshest fish available. If you aren't in the habit of
making fish stews, definitely try this one. It's easy, it's full of flavor,

it cooks a lot faster than any other kind of stew, and it tastes wonderful on a cold winter afternoon. I've been making this for the Super Bowl the past few years, and it always disappears!

Serves 4

1 tablespoon olive oil
¼ pound pearl onions, peeled
4 garlic cloves, minced
1 28-ounce can whole peeled tomatoes, drained
1 14-ounce can artichoke hearts, drained
1 roasted red bell pepper, page 85, diced
2½ cups chardonnay
2 tablespoons chopped fresh cilantro
Sea salt and freshly ground pepper
1 tablespoon drained capers
¼ teaspoon dried oregano
1½ pounds white-fleshed, mild fish fillets, such as cod, mahimahi, sole, or halibut, cut into large bite-size chunks

1. Preheat the oven to 350°F.

2. In a wok or large skillet, heat ½ tablespoon of the oil over medium heat. Add the onions and garlic, and sauté for 2 to 3 minutes, or until the onions are lightly browned. Take care the garlic does not burn.

3. Add the tomatoes, artichoke hearts, roasted pepper, and chardonnay and stir. Add the cilantro, and season to taste with salt and black pepper. Bring the contents to a simmer over medium-high heat, adjust the heat to maintain the simmer, cover, and cook for 20 minutes. Add the capers and oregano, taste, and adjust the seasoning.

4. Meanwhile, in another skillet, heat the remaining ½ tablespoon oil over medium-high heat. Add the fish to the pan and sauté for 3 to 4 minutes, or until cooked halfway through and lightly browned.

Transfer the fillets to a shallow baking dish large enough to hold them in a single layer.

5. Pour the tomato mixture over the fish and bake for about 20 minutes, until the fish is cooked through and the liquid is bubbling. Serve at once.

Per serving: 19 grams carbohydrates, 28 grams protein, 3.5 grams fat

Steamed Arctic Char

The first time I had arctic char, I was in Toronto, and my husband and I shared a whole fish and were enchanted by the moist texture and exquisite flavor. If you can't find the red fish, salmon will do, but see if your fish merchant can get char for you. You will love it! Use a bamboo steamer or another flat steaming basket for the best effect, and try not to use too much water when you steam the fish; you don't want it to splash on the fish. I keep this recipe simple so that the full flavor of the fish shines through. Serve with steamed asparagus and Summer Cherries Jubilee on page 262.

Serves 4

1½ pounds arctic char or salmon, cut into 4 equal-size pieces, each
    about ¾ inch thick
4 tablespoons snipped fresh dill
2 teaspoons grated fresh ginger
Herbamare or sea salt and freshly ground pepper
1 lemon

1. Lay the fish in the steaming basket of a bamboo fish steamer or other steamer, and sprinkle with dill, ginger, and Herbamare to taste.

2. Slice the lemon in 6 slices, and then cut each slice in half. Lay them evenly on top of the fish.

3. Set the steaming basket over boiling water, reduce the heat to medium so that the water simmers, cover the steamer, and steam for about 4 minutes, until the fish is cooked through and opaque in the center. Serve.

Per serving: 0 grams carbohydrates, 28 grams protein, 0 grams fat

Sautéed Calamari with Garlic and Onion

Although I give you the choice of using two, three, or four cloves of garlic, I admit that I crave a lot of garlic with calamari and so always go for the maximum! You may not be as much of a garlic hound, but if you like slightly salty, pleasingly chewy calamari, you'll be delighted by this recipe. The trick to preparing calamari or squid is to keep the cooking to a bare minimum—in this case, 3 minutes. (If you braise or stew it, cook it for about 10 minutes.) Overcooking only results in rubbery calamari, and that's a shame. To keep this in the Zone, serve it with asparagus and spaghetti squash and a glass of a nice chilled white wine.

Serves 4

1 tablespoon olive oil
1 large white or red onion, sliced
2 to 4 garlic cloves, crushed
8 ounces bottled clam juice
½ cup dry vermouth or dry white wine

2 anchovies, finely chopped

Hot red pepper sauce or crushed red chili pepper

1½ pounds cleaned, fresh or frozen and thawed calamari, cut into ¼-inch-thick rings

3 tablespoons chopped flat-leaf parsley

1. In a nonstick frying pan, heat the olive oil over medium heat. Add the onion and cook for 2 minutes to soften slightly. Add the garlic and sauté for 1 to 2 minutes, until the onion is translucent and the garlic softens without coloring.

2. Add the clam juice and bring the contents to a boil. Reduce the heat to a simmer, add the vermouth and anchovies, and season to taste with hot sauce. Return the contents to a simmer, and cook for about 15 minutes, until the flavors blend.

3. Raise the heat to medium-high and add the calamari. Cook for about 3 minutes, add the parsley, and cook for another minute or so, until the calamari rings are cooked through. Be careful not to overcook. Serve the calamari with the pan sauce.

Per serving: 4 grams carbohydrates, 28 grams protein, 3.5 grams fat

Asian Steamed Catfish with Vegetables

Fish is great cooked in a bamboo steamer. The catfish fillets take about 15 minutes, during which time the water can evaporate, so check the water level periodically. You could also use thinner fish, such as trout, and reduce the cooking time to 7 or 8 minutes. Just

about any mild, white-fleshed fish fillet works for this recipe. Asian flavors such as those here—ginger, hoisin sauce, mirin, and sesame oil—seem just right with the steamed fish and the vegetables.

Serves 2

12 ounces catfish fillets
2 teaspoons grated fresh ginger
2 leeks, or 4 scallions, white and green parts, thinly sliced diagonally
Sea salt
⅓ cup diced butternut squash
3 cups chopped bok choy (about ¾ pound)
1 cup halved white or cremini mushrooms
2 tablespoons hoisin sauce
1 tablespoon mirin
1 teaspoon toasted sesame oil
2 tablespoons toasted sesame seeds (see note on page 167)

1. Put the fish in a bamboo steaming basket or other fish steamer. Sprinkle the ginger and leeks over the fish, and season lightly with salt.

2. Put the squash and bok choy in another steaming basket.

3. Set the vegetable steamer in a larger pan filled partway with boiling water, cover, and steam for 15 minutes. Add the mushrooms, and steam for about 5 minutes longer, until the vegetables are tender.

4. Set the bamboo steamer in a larger pan filled partway with boiling water, cover, and steam for 10 to 15 minutes, or until the fish is opaque. The timing depends on the thickness of the fillets.

5. Meanwhile, in a small bowl, stir together the hoisin sauce, mirin, and sesame oil.

6. Transfer the fish to a serving platter. Spread the hoisin sauce over the fish, and sprinkle with sesame seeds. Serve immediately with the steamed vegetables.

Per serving: 36 grams carbohydrates, 26 grams protein, 2 grams fat

---

Zone Tip

Steaming is a technique used throughout Asia, where home cooks prefer bamboo steamers. I'm with them. These stackable, inexpensive tools are the best for steaming, far better than the flimsy steaming baskets (which I pretty much dismiss as useless) so many people have to insert in various pots and pans. For my uses, bamboo is better than a sturdy metal steamer. Bamboo steamers, which are about nine inches in diameter, are sold in most cookware stores. When you're ready to steam your food, set the steamer in a skillet or another flat pan that is a little wider than the steamer, and fill the skillet partway with boiling water. When you are done, wash the steamer in the sink with soap and warm water, and let it air-dry; do not put it in the dishwasher. Of course, you may prefer a good metal steamer instead. Your choice.

Sautéed Trout with Lemon and Garlic

Every so often I see trout in the market, and when I do, I buy it immediately. It's a slightly oily freshwater fish with a lovely flavor. If you're lucky enough to have an angler in the family, you might get to enjoy fresh-caught wild brook trout, which is one of the finest of culinary treats. Here, I cook it simply with just a little lemon, some garlic, and a finish of fresh dill. For a Zone-favorable meal, serve with roasted vegetables and ½ cup of blueberries.

Serves 4

2 teaspoons olive oil
1 large garlic clove, crushed
1½ pounds boneless trout fillet or haddock, cod, or other white-
    fleshed fish fillets
Herbamare
3 tablespoons snipped fresh dill
Pinch of mild chili powder*
Juice of 1 lemon

1. In a skillet, heat the olive oil over medium-high heat. Add the garlic and cook for about 1 minute, until it's softened but not colored.

2. Season the trout lightly with Herbamare and add it to the skillet. Cook for 4 minutes, or until the trout begins to firm up and cook through. Turn, and season evenly with dill and chili powder. Cook for 2 to 3 minutes longer, or until the fish is opaque and flakes easily. During the last minute of cooking, add the lemon juice. Serve immediately.

Per serving: 0 grams carbohydrates, 28 grams protein, 3.5 grams fat

*I like Santa Fe School Chimayo Style Chile Powder, which I order online at santafeschoolofcooking.com. I also like Emeril's Southwest Seasoning.

$\mathcal{P}$oultry and Meat

Hoisin Barbecued Chicken

Simple is the word that comes to mind when I think of making this succulent grilled chicken. I always keep hoisin sauce in my refrigerator, and everything else—the ginger, garlic, orange juice, and fruit spread—is usually ready and waiting, too. Once you mix up the marinade, you can let the chicken marinate for hours until you're ready to grill it. *Simple* will be the word you come up with, too! I like to marinate the chicken in a plastic bag, because it makes the process easier than ever, and I can fit the bag into the fridge without having to clear out too much other food. If you can, buy free-range, antibiotic-free chicken. Serve this with salad, string beans, and The Best Applesauce on page 259.

Serves 4

4 tablespoons hoisin sauce
3 tablespoons orange juice
2 tablespoons dry vermouth
1 tablespoon sugar-free apricot fruit spread
1½ teaspoons shredded or grated fresh ginger
1 garlic clove, minced
4 boneless, skinless chicken breast halves, each about 4 ounces
Vegetable oil cooking spray

1. In a small bowl, stir together the hoisin sauce, orange juice, vermouth, apricot spread, ginger, and garlic.

2. Put the chicken in a large plastic zip bag or a shallow, nonreactive dish. Pour the marinade over the chicken. Shake the bag to coat the chicken, or turn the chicken several times in the dish. Refrigerate for at least 1 hour and up to 12 hours.

3. Prepare a charcoal or gas grill. Coat the grill rack with vegetable oil cooking spray. The coals or heating elements are ready when they are medium-hot.

4. Remove the chicken from the bag or dish, letting most of the marinade drip off, and transfer it to the grill. Grill the chicken, turning once or twice, for 8 to 10 minutes, or until cooked through.

5. Meanwhile, pour the leftover marinade into a small saucepan and bring it to a rapid boil over high heat. Reduce the heat slightly, and boil gently for 5 full minutes.

6. Transfer the chicken to a serving platter and pour the marinade over it. Serve immediately.

Per serving: 19 grams carbohydrates, 26 grams protein, 0 grams fat

---

Zone Tip

"Zone proof" your kitchen. Discard all the pasta, white rice, white flour, white sugar, pancake and cake mixes, and bread. Replace them with healthful, Zone-favorable carbohydrates such as steel-cut oats, barley, beans, wild rice, and brown rice.

Chicken with Asparagus

This dish includes a few of my very favorite foods: asparagus, portobello mushrooms, and sweet cherry tomatoes. Because the flavors and textures sing so well together, this is one of my family's most-requested dinners. Double the amount of chicken without adding more oil or broth, if you want, and add more vegetables to increase the carbohydrates. Or, enjoy it with a glass of chilled white wine and some fresh fruit for dessert.

Serves 2

2 boneless, skinless chicken breast halves, each about 4 ounces, cut
into 1-inch chunks
Herbamare
Coarse salt and freshly ground pepper
Olive oil cooking spray
1 tablespoon olive oil
8 medium asparagus spears, cut into 2-inch-long pieces
4 cherry tomatoes, halved
4 teardrop tomatoes, halved (use cherry tomatoes if you can't find
teardrops)
1 large portobello mushroom, stem and gills removed, cut into 8 to
10 1-inch pieces
6 scallions, white part only, sliced diagonally
3 large garlic cloves, thinly sliced
¼ cup low-sodium chicken broth
3 tablespoons dry white wine
3 tablespoons fresh lemon juice
2 tablespoons minced fresh basil

1. Season the chicken lightly on both sides with Herbamare, salt, and
pepper, and set aside.

2. Coat a sauté pan with olive oil cooking spray. Put 1 teaspoon of
the olive oil in the pan, and heat it over medium heat. Add the
asparagus, cherry and teardrop tomatoes, and mushroom, and cook,
stirring occasionally, for 4 to 5 minutes, or until the tomatoes soften.
Add the scallions and cook, stirring, for 2 minutes longer, or until
softened. Transfer the vegetables to a bowl.

3. Heat another teaspoon of the olive oil in the pan, add the
chicken, and cook for 1 minute, or until it begins to brown on one
side. Turn the chicken with a spatula, and cook for about 5 minutes
longer, stirring and turning, until the meat is evenly browned.
Transfer the chicken to the bowl with the vegetables.

4. Spray the pan again with cooking spray. Put the remaining teaspoon of olive oil in the pan, add the garlic, and sauté for about 1 minute, until golden. Stir in the chicken broth, wine, and lemon juice, and bring the contents to a boil. Reduce the heat and simmer for 3 minutes. Use a wooden spoon to scrape up any brown bits stuck to the bottom of the pan and mix them into the broth. Reduce the heat to medium-low and stir well.

5. Stir the chicken and vegetables into the pan and cook, stirring gently, until heated through. Stir in the basil, season to taste with more salt and pepper, and serve.

Per serving: 12 grams carbohydrates, 26 grams protein, 7 grams fat

Zone Tip
Keep a good set of wooden spoons in your kitchen. They stand up to the heat and do not scratch pans.

Chicken and Snow Pea Stir-Fry

Just about everyone has a fondness for stir-fries, and I am right there in the crowd! Instead of serving this over rice, I like to serve it with spaghetti squash. You'll be charmed if you do, and you won't eat all those unnecessary carbohydrates. I make this with chicken, but you can substitute another protein, such as shrimp, scallops, or very lean beef. And when it comes to the vegetables, try bok choy, asparagus, or zucchini instead of snow peas, broccoli, or cauliflower. Have about a half cup of fresh pineapple for dessert and stay in the Zone.

Serves 4

1 small head broccoli (about ¾ pound)
½ head cauliflower (about ¾ pound)
1 tablespoon peanut oil or olive oil
1 tablespoon minced garlic
1 tablespoon minced fresh ginger
1 pound boneless, skinless chicken breasts, cut into 16 chunks
2 carrots, cut into matchsticks
¼ cup low-sodium chicken broth
1 red bell pepper, cut into matchsticks
1 pound fresh snow peas, trimmed
3 tablespoons low-sodium soy sauce
1 teaspoon toasted sesame oil
Pinch or more of crushed hot red pepper flakes, optional

1. Trim the broccoli and cauliflower, and remove and discard the thick stalks. Slice the florets into 1-inch pieces and set aside.

2. Heat a wok or deep skillet over high heat. Pour in the peanut oil, and when it's hot and shimmering, add the garlic and ginger, and toss for about 20 seconds, until fragrant but not colored. Add the chicken, and stir-fry for 2 to 3 minutes, or until the meat turns white. Using a slotted spoon, transfer the chicken, garlic, and ginger to a bowl and set it aside.

3. Add the broccoli, cauliflower, carrots, and 1 tablespoon of the chicken broth to the wok. Add a little more oil, if necessary, to prevent sticking. Stir-fry for 3 to 4 minutes, or until the vegetables are crisp and tender. Push the vegetables up the sides of the wok.

4. Add the bell pepper and 1 more tablespoon of the chicken broth, and stir-fry for about 1 minute, until the pepper begins to soften.

5. Return the chicken mixture to the wok and add the snow peas. Push the other vegetables to the center of the wok, and stir-fry all the ingredients for about 1 minute, until the chicken is cooked through.

6. Add the remaining 2 tablespoons of chicken broth, the soy sauce, and the sesame oil. Season with pepper flakes, if desired. Stir-fry for about 30 seconds longer, until piping hot. Serve immediately.

Per serving: 17 grams carbohydrates, 26 grams protein, 4.5 grams fat

> ### Zone Tip
> Stir-fries don't have to use oil—or at least very much. Chicken or vegetable broth will moisten the food just fine and keep the fat content down. A nonstick skillet or wok is a worthwhile investment, too, if you like stir-fries.

Chicken in Lemon and Green Olive Sauce

Green olives and lemon juice mingle with the chicken, garlic, onion, and broth for a lovely, distinctive dish that, if you like olives, will earn your applause. I prefer the organic chicken broth sold in cartons that can be refrigerated for several days. Pair this with steamed squash, asparagus, and a salad, and end the meal with a serving of The Best Applesauce on page 259.

Serves 4

2 teaspoons olive oil
1 large yellow onion, finely diced
3 garlic cloves, minced
¼ cup crushed or coarsely chopped pitted green olives
Sea salt and freshly ground pepper or Herbamare
4 boneless, skinless chicken breast halves, each about 4 ounces

1 cup low-sodium chicken broth
Juice of 1½ lemons (approximately ⅓ cup)
¼ cup finely chopped flat-leaf parsley or cilantro

1. In a nonstick skillet large enough to hold the chicken in a single layer or slightly overlapping, heat the olive oil over medium heat. Add the onion and cook for about 2 minutes, until it begins to soften. Add the garlic and olives, and cook 1 to 2 minutes longer, or until the onion colors slightly. Season to taste with salt and pepper, and then transfer the contents to a small bowl and set it aside.

2. Put the chicken in the pan, raise the heat to medium-high, and sauté for 4 to 5 minutes on each side, turning once, until the meat is golden brown on both sides. Return the onion mixture to the pan and cook, stirring the vegetables around the chicken, for about 1 minute, until integrated. Add the chicken broth and lemon juice, and bring the contents to a boil. Lower the heat a little, and stir in the parsley.

3. Reduce the heat to low, cover, and cook for about 15 minutes, until the chicken is cooked through.

Per serving: 5 grams carbohydrates, 26 grams protein, 4.5 grams fat

Zone Tip
A good way to add diversity and interest to your daily diet is to try new recipes. I get excited just thinking about trying something for the first time. Make it a goal to experiment with a different recipe or "exotic" food at least once a week.

Mustard Chicken with Grapes

I came up with this mustard-based marinade for bone-in chicken breasts one day, and then when I cooked the chicken, I decided to plunk some grapes into the baking dish. Wow! As the grapes heat, they get sweeter and juicier and then mix with the chicken and pan juices in a delightful medley of flavors and textures. I often cook boneless, skinless chicken breasts, but in this recipe I like bone-in breasts, with the skin removed to cut back on the fat. To complete this Zone-favorable meal, serve lightly sautéed mixed vegetables and some butternut squash.

Serves 4

Olive oil cooking spray
¼ cup fresh lime juice
3 tablespoons Dijon mustard
1 teaspoon Splenda
½ teaspoon grated lime zest
½ teaspoon crushed fresh rosemary
½ teaspoon cracked pepper
4 bone-in, skinless chicken breast halves
2 cups white or red seedless grapes
Herbamare
Sea salt

1. Lightly coat a shallow baking dish large enough to hold the chicken in a single layer, or slightly overlapping, with olive oil cooking spray.

2. In a small bowl, stir together the lime juice, mustard, Splenda, lime zest, rosemary, and pepper. Lay the chicken in a shallow, nonreactive dish and pour the mustard marinade over it. Turn the chicken several times to coat it evenly, and let it marinate at room temperature for 15 minutes. (You can also cover the dish and

refrigerate the chicken for up to 6 hours; then take the chicken from the refrigerator while the oven heats to bring it to room temperature.)

3. Preheat the oven to 350°F. Lift the chicken from the marinade, letting most of the liquid drip back into the dish and scraping the excess off the chicken, and arrange the pieces in the baking dish. Reserve the marinade.

4. Bake for 15 minutes, and then pull the pan from the oven and brush the chicken with the marinade. Bake for 15 minutes longer. Again, pull the pan from the oven, turn the chicken, and brush the other side with the remaining marinade. Add the grapes to the pan, distributing them around the chicken, and bake about 15 minutes longer, or until the chicken is cooked through.

5. Brush the chicken and grapes with the pan juices, and serve immediately.

Per serving: 9 grams carbohydrates, 28 grams protein, 0 grams fat

Sesame-Orange Chicken

The marinade for this bone-in chicken is a lovely blending of Asian flavors sweetened ever so slightly with Splenda. When you lift the chicken from the marinade, let most of the liquid drip back into the dish, and then be sure not to crowd the pieces in the baking pan so that they cook evenly. I boil the leftover marinade for two impor- tant reasons: first, boiling thickens it and concentrates its flavors; and second, cooking destroys any harmful bacteria that could be lurking in the marinade after its close association with the raw chicken. Round out this meal with steamed asparagus and cauliflower and some of The Best Applesauce on page 259.

Serves 4

⅓ cup orange juice
1½ tablespoons low-sodium soy sauce
1 tablespoon Splenda
1 tablespoon toasted sesame oil
½ tablespoon minced fresh ginger
1 teaspoon finely minced garlic
⅛ teaspoon crushed red pepper flakes
Grated zest of 2 oranges
1 pound bone-in, skinless chicken breast halves, 4 ounces each
Sea salt and freshly ground pepper
4 scallions, white and green parts, sliced diagonally
2 tablespoons sesame seeds, toasted*

1. In a small bowl, stir together the orange juice, soy sauce, Splenda, sesame oil, ginger, garlic, pepper flakes, and orange zest. Lay the chicken in a shallow, nonreactive dish and pour the marinade over it. Turn the chicken several times to coat evenly. Cover the dish and refrigerate the chicken for at least 6 hours and up to 12 hours. Let the chicken return to room temperature before cooking.

2. Preheat the oven to 375°F.

3. Lift the chicken pieces from the marinade, letting most of the liquid drip back into the dish and scraping the excess off the chicken, and arrange them in a baking dish in a single layer or slightly overlapping. Pour about a third of the remaining marinade over the chicken, and reserve the rest for the orange sauce. Sprinkle the chicken lightly with salt and pepper, and bake for about 45 minutes to 1 hour, until cooked through.

4. About 10 minutes before the chicken is done, strain the reserved marinade into a small saucepan, bring it to a boil over medium-high

heat, and cook, stirring, for 8 to 10 minutes, or until slightly thickened.

5. Transfer the chicken to a serving platter and drizzle the hot orange sauce over it. Garnish with scallions and sesame seeds, and serve.

*To toast sesame seeds, spread the seeds in a single layer in a small skillet. Shaking the pan, toast the seeds over medium heat for 30 seconds to 1 minute, or until they darken a shade and become fragrant and a few "pop." Immediately transfer the seeds to a plate to stop the cooking.

Per serving: 3 grams carbohydrates, 26 grams protein, 5 grams fat

Chicken and Peppers with Black Bean and Garlic Sauce

This recipe uses a few more pans than some of the others, but the extra effort is definitely rewarded. In the end, the chicken and vegetables are cooked on top of the stove in a flameproof casserole, and the whole thing comes together beautifully. The fermented black beans, sold in Asian markets and some supermarkets, impart a uniquely pungent and salty flavor. (For more on these beans, turn to page 106.) I call for cornstarch here to thicken the sauce, but if you have arrowroot, use it instead. Arrowroot, which is easier to digest and has no carbs, provides a lovely sheen but does not hold up to reheating. Serve with a salad, ¼ cup of brown rice, and sliced pineapple for dessert.

Serves 4

½ cup low-sodium chicken broth
¼ cup sherry
2 tablespoons salted black beans, rinsed, drained, and mashed
2 tablespoons low-sodium soy sauce
¼ teaspoon Splenda, fructose, or honey
⅛ teaspoon grated fresh ginger
1 tablespoon plus 1 teaspoon toasted sesame oil
1 large yellow onion, halved lengthwise and cut into ¼-inch slices
3 garlic cloves, minced
1 pound boneless, skinless chicken breasts, cut into 1-inch pieces
1 green bell pepper, sliced into ¼- to ½-inch-wide slices
1 red bell pepper, sliced into ¼- to ½-inch-wide slices
1 head bok choy, halved lengthwise and cut into ½-inch-thick slices
2 teaspoons cornstarch
2 teaspoons cold water
½ cup lightly beaten egg whites (3 to 4 whites)

1. In a 4-quart flame proof casserole or saucepan, stir together the chicken broth, sherry, black beans, soy sauce, Splenda, and ginger, and bring to a boil over medium-high heat. Remove from the heat.

2. Heat a large skillet or wok over high heat. Pour 1 tablespoon of the sesame oil into the pan and swirl the pan to coat the cooking surface. Add the onion, and stir-fry for 2 minutes, or until it begins to soften. Add the garlic, and stir-fry for about 1 minute, until softened but not colored. Add the chicken, and stir-fry for 6 to 8 minutes, until the chicken is lightly browned.

3. Using a slotted spoon so that the oil can drain, transfer the chicken and onion to the casserole. Bring the contents of the casserole to a boil over high heat, reduce the heat to medium-low so that the liquid simmers, cover, and cook for 40 minutes, adjusting the heat to maintain the simmer.

4. Add the green and red bell peppers and the bok choy to the casserole, and stir to mix well, making sure any pieces of chicken on the bottom of the pan are brought to the top. Re-cover and simmer for 10 to 15 minutes longer.

5. Meanwhile, in a small bowl, whisk the cornstarch with the water, and stir it into the casserole to thicken the sauce slightly.

6. Stir in the egg whites and cook just long enough for the whites to coagulate. Drizzle with the remaining teaspoon of sesame oil and serve immediately.

Per serving: 9 grams carbohydrates, 27 grams protein, 3.5 grams fat

Southwestern Chicken

Just about everyone likes the sunny, bold flavors of the Southwest, and this dish takes full advantage of those flavors. Even the tiny bit of cinnamon contributes to the authentic flavor. I'm partial to medium Chimayo Style Chile Powder, which is a mild chili powder that I buy online from the Santa Fe School of Cooking. I get a 12-ounce can and store it in the freezer, where it keeps for months. It pays to look around for a good chili powder because the mass-market brands sold in supermarkets often pale in comparison. Plus, it's fun to sample different types, and you would be surprised how different they are. Serve this with Brazilian Black Beans, page 234, a tossed green salad, and ½ cup of fresh pineapple.

Serves 4

1½ teaspoons olive oil
1 yellow onion, thinly sliced

½ red bell pepper, sliced into ½-inch-wide strips
½ green bell pepper, sliced into ½-inch-wide strips
1 garlic clove
2 tablespoons orange juice
2 tablespoons white or red wine
2 tablespoons mild chili powder or mild paprika
1 tablespoon water
¾ teaspoon dried oregano
¼ teaspoon ground cinnamon
¼ teaspoon crushed hot red pepper flakes
¼ teaspoon ground coriander, optional
¼ teaspoon sea salt or Spicy Herbamare
1 pound boneless, skinless chicken breast halves, 4 ounces each
Lime wedges

1. In a nonstick skillet large enough to hold the chicken pieces in a single layer or slightly overlapping, heat the olive oil over medium heat. Add the onion and red and green bell peppers, and cook for about 5 minutes, until the vegetables begin to soften.

2. In a food processor fitted with the metal blade, combine the garlic, orange juice, wine, chili powder, water, oregano, cinnamon, pepper flakes, coriander, if using, and salt. Process to a smooth paste.

3. Add the chicken to the skillet and spread half of the paste over the pieces. Sauté over medium-high heat for 10 minutes. Turn the chicken, and spread the rest of the paste over the other side. Cook for 10 minutes longer, or until the chicken is cooked through. Serve garnished with lime wedges.

Per serving: 2 grams carbohydrates, 28 grams protein, 2 grams fat

Chicken Cacciatore

The warm, rich flavors of chicken cacciatore are always welcome but never more so than on a cool fall evening. This version of the classic stew is easy to put together and is ready in about an hour, time enough for you to make a big salad with grated carrots and the Whipped Cauliflower on page 241. Serve seasonal fruit for dessert, such as apples or pears.

Serves 4

1 tablespoon olive oil
1 pound boneless, skinless chicken breasts, cut into 1-inch pieces
1 yellow onion, sliced
1 green bell pepper, chopped
1 garlic clove, minced
1 1-pound can Italian-style diced tomatoes
2 tablespoons chopped flat-leaf parsley, plus additional parsley for
    garnish
¼ teaspoon dried oregano
¼ teaspoon dried thyme
¾ teaspoon Herbamare or sea salt
Freshly ground black pepper
4 ounces mushrooms, sliced (about 3 cups)
¼ cup dry white wine

1. In a large nonstick skillet, heat the olive oil over medium-high heat. Add the chicken and cook for 5 to 6 minutes, turning, until lightly browned. Remove the chicken from the pan and set it aside.

2. Put the onion, bell pepper, and garlic in the skillet and cook 3 to 4 minutes, or until the onion is softened but not colored. Add the tomatoes, 2 tablespoons parsley, oregano, thyme, and Herbamare. Season to taste with black pepper.

3. Reduce the heat to medium-low so that the liquid simmers, and cook for about 15 minutes, stirring occasionally. Add the chicken, cover the skillet, and simmer for 45 minutes, stirring occasionally. Adjust the heat in order to maintain the simmer.

4. Add the mushrooms and wine, and stir gently. Cook uncovered for about 15 minutes, until the sauce is the desired consistency. Serve garnished with parsley.

Per serving: 9.5 grams carbohydrates, 26 grams protein, 3.5 grams fat

Chicken Stir-Fry with Almonds

When Asian cooks prepare a stir-fry, they spend a lot of time prepping the ingredients so that each is ready to be added to the hot pan on a second's notice. French chefs do the same thing and call the prepped ingredients their *mise en place*, which means everything is in place and ready to go. So, grate the ginger, crush the garlic, and slice the chicken for this stir-fry, and get ready to enjoy an easy meal. Take care not to overcook the fowl. Serve with a salad, wild rice, and sliced oranges for dessert.

Serves 4

2 teaspoons olive oil
1 teaspoon grated fresh ginger
3 garlic cloves, crushed
1 pound boneless, skinless chicken breasts, cut into 1-inch-thick strips
3 cups low-sodium chicken broth
1 cup diced bamboo shoots
1 cup diced celery

1 cup diced bok choy
½ cup drained and sliced water chestnuts
¼ cup blanched almonds
2 tablespoons low-sodium soy sauce
1 teaspoon Herbamare
2 tablespoons arrowroot or cornstarch
¼ cup water

1. In a wok or large skillet, heat the oil over medium heat. Add the
ginger and garlic, and cook for about 1 minute, until softened but
not colored.

2. Add the chicken and cook, stirring, for about 3 minutes. Add the
chicken broth, bamboo shoots, celery, bok choy, water chestnuts,
almonds, soy sauce, and Herbamare, and cook, stirring, for 1 minute.
Cover tightly and cook for 4 minutes.

3. Meanwhile, in a small bowl, stir together the arrowroot and
water until smooth. Add to the skillet and cook, stirring constantly,
until the mixture thickens. Adjust the seasoning with Herbamare and
serve immediately.

Per serving: 21 grams carbohydrates, 26 grams protein, 6 grams fat

Chicken Stir-Fry with Collard Greens

Greens such as collards and Swiss chard are high in calcium and rich
in antioxidants. Best of all, you can eat cups and cups of the dark
greens and never exceed your carbohydrate limit. They wilt readily

when cooked, similarly to spinach, and taste great with the chicken. The toasted sesame oil provides a nice hint of nutty flavor. Serve with Tangy Coleslaw, page 97, half a small sweet potato, and Microwave Apple, page 258, for dessert.

Serves 4

2 teaspoons olive oil
2 garlic cloves, minced
1 teaspoon grated fresh ginger
1 sweet onion, such as Vidalia or Maui, diced
3 cups roughly sliced collard greens or Swiss chard
1 pound boneless, skinless chicken breasts, cut into 1-inch pieces
Dry sherry or chicken broth, optional
Low-sodium tamari or soy sauce
1 teaspoon toasted sesame oil

1. In a wok or large skillet, heat 1 teaspoon of the olive oil over medium heat. Add the garlic and ginger, and cook for about 1 minute, until softened but not colored. Add the onion and cook for about 5 minutes, until softened. Add the collard greens, sprinkle them with just a little water so that it clings to the leaves, and cook, stirring, for about 10 minutes, until wilted. Lift the greens from the pan and set them aside.

2. Add the remaining teaspoon of olive oil to the pan, raise the heat to medium-high, and add the chicken. Cook the chicken for 6 to 8 minutes, turning a few times, until lightly browned on all sides and cooked through. If the chicken needs some moisture, add a tablespoon or two of sherry or broth to the pan.

3. Return the collards to the pan, add the tamari and sesame oil, and mix well. Cook just until heated through, and serve.

Per serving: 4 grams carbohydrates, 26 grams protein, 3.5 grams fat

Grilled Chicken and Fennel with Spicy Orange Glaze

I was inspired to create this easy grilled-chicken recipe after seeing a similar one in a magazine. I made it Zone friendly, of course. The taste of the grilled fennel is a perfect complement to the chicken. Serve with a salad and orange slices for a Zone-favorable meal.

Serves 4

2 cups orange juice
1 cinnamon stick
½ teaspoon crushed hot red pepper flakes
Vegetable oil cooking spray
3 medium fennel bulbs
4 boneless, skinless chicken breast halves, each about 4 ounces
1 tablespoon olive oil
Sea salt

1. In a saucepan, combine the orange juice, cinnamon stick, and red pepper flakes, and bring to a boil over high heat. Reduce the heat to medium-high and simmer briskly for 12 to 15 minutes, or until the mixture is syrupy and reduced to about ½ cup. Remove and discard the cinnamon stick. Cover the sauce and set aside.

2. Prepare a charcoal or gas grill. Coat the grill rack with vegetable oil cooking spray. The coals or heating elements are ready when they are medium-hot.

3. Cut off and discard the stalks and tough outer layers of the fennel bulbs. Set each bulb upright and cut it into ½-inch-thick pieces by slicing from the top nearly to the core. Each piece will somewhat resemble a fan.

4. Line a tray with wax paper, and arrange the fennel slices and breast halves on it in a single layer. Whisk the olive oil into the reserved orange glaze. Brush both sides of the chicken and fennel with glaze, and sprinkle lightly with salt.

5. Grill the chicken and fennel for about 10 minutes, turning once, until the chicken is cooked through and both are nicely seared with grill marks.

Per serving: 28 grams carbohydrates, 26 grams protein, 3.5 grams fat

Lemon-and-Herb-Grilled Chicken and Vegetables

This marinade works like magic on both the chicken and the vegetables. You can be creative when it comes to the vegetables you choose, but just be sure to have plenty, because I have learned that there's hardly a soul who doesn't gobble them up! To make this a complete Zone meal, I grill some fresh pineapple, which gets lovely grill marks on it, and add a small side dish of wild rice (about ⅕ cup).

Serves 4

1 cup fresh lemon juice
½ cup olive oil
4 tablespoons chopped flat-leaf parsley
6 garlic cloves, finely chopped
2 tablespoons snipped fresh dill or chopped rosemary or tarragon
½ teaspoon freshly ground pepper
Herbamare
4 boneless, skinless chicken breast halves, each about 4 ounces

6 small zucchini, cut lengthwise
6 small summer squashes, cut lengthwise
3 large white onions, halved
6 bell peppers (2 green, 2 red, 2 yellow), quartered*

1. In a small bowl, stir together the lemon juice, olive oil, parsley, garlic, dill, and black pepper. Season to taste with Herbamare.

2. Put the chicken in a large plastic zip bag. Put the pieces of zucchini, squash, onion, and bell pepper in another bag. Divide the marinade between the two bags. Seal the bags, turn them over to make sure the contents are coated, and refrigerate for at least 6 hours and up to 12 hours, turning them periodically.

3. Prepare a charcoal or gas grill. Lay a sheet of aluminum foil over the grill rack to keep the chicken and vegetables from burning. The coals or heating elements are ready when they are medium-hot.

4. Lift the vegetables from the plastic bag, letting any excess marinade drip back into the bag, and transfer them to the grill. Reserve the marinade. Cook for about 30 minutes total; the squash may cook faster than the onions, and the onions may be done before the peppers. Watch carefully, and turn the vegetables several times and brush them with the marinade during grilling. Transfer the grilled vegetables to a platter. (If cooking on a charcoal fire, check to see if you should add more coals to the fire to keep it medium-hot while you cook the chicken.)

5. Lift the breast halves from the plastic bag, letting any excess marinade drip back into the bag, and transfer them to the grill. Discard the marinade. Cook for 6 to 7 minutes on each side, turning once.

6. Serve the chicken and vegetables together.

Per serving: 27 grams carbohydrates, 26 grams protein, 14 grams fat

*You can use any color of bell peppers you want. Have a merry mixture of colors or use only one or two. It's your choice and taste preference (all are high in vitamin C), limited only by what is available in your market—or garden!

Citrus-Ginger Roast Chicken

Roasting the whole bird is one of the easiest and homiest ways to serve chicken. As it cooks, the house fills with comforting aromas, and everyone is more than ready for dinner when it's time to eat. You will have to eyeball the portion size to stay in the Zone— if you need help, eat only enough meat to match the thickness and size of your palm. Be sure to remove and discard the chicken skin, and favor white meat over dark meat, which is higher in fat. Round out this meal with a mesclun salad mixed with a few dried cranberries, and salute the cook with a glass of red wine. Have Poached Pears, page 260, or The Best Applesauce, page 259, for dessert.

Serves 8

1 5-pound roasting chicken
1 orange, plus additional orange sections for garnish
2 lemons
3 tablespoons finely grated fresh ginger
Sea salt, optional
Freshly ground pepper
Herbamare
½ cup fresh orange juice
¼ cup fresh lemon juice
3 tablespoons Splenda
2 teaspoons olive oil

1. Preheat the oven to 350°F.

2. Rinse the inside and outside of the chicken under cool, running water. Pat dry with paper towels.

3. Grate the zest of the orange and one of the lemons. Reserve both the zests. Cut the orange and both lemons into quarters.

4. Rub the outside of the chicken with the zested lemon quarters and then discard them. In a small bowl, mix together the zests and 1 tablespoon of the ginger. Rub the mixture evenly in the cavity of the chicken.

5. Insert the citrus quarters in the cavity of the chicken. Season the chicken inside and out with salt, if using, pepper, and Herbamare. Transfer the chicken to a rack set in a roasting pan.

6. In a bowl, stir together the orange and lemon juices, Splenda, olive oil, and the remaining 2 tablespoons of ginger, and keep it at hand for basting.

7. Roast the chicken on the middle rack of the oven for 1½ to 2 hours, or until an instant-read thermometer inserted in the fleshy part of the thigh registers 170°F and the juices run clear.

8. Transfer the chicken to a platter, and let it rest for 10 minutes before removing and discarding the skin and carving the meat. Serve garnished with orange sections.

Per serving: 9 grams carbohydrates, 28 grams protein, 3.5 grams fat

Roast Chicken Rolls Stuffed with Sun-Dried Tomatoes, Spinach, and Goat Cheese

These elegant and tasty little chicken rolls take some planning and effort, but they are spectacular. You will want to serve them for your next dinner party—and you will deserve the raves you'll get! It's easy to pound the chicken breasts, but you could ask the butcher to do it for you. I like to season the breasts the night before for maximum flavor and also because it makes it just a little easier to complete the dish the next day. Serve steamed zucchini as a side dish and Poached Pears, page 260, for dessert to complete the meal.

Serves 4

⅓ cup sun-dried tomatoes
4 boneless, skinless chicken breast halves, each about 3½ ounces
4 garlic cloves, chopped
Herbamare
Sea salt and freshly ground pepper
1 tablespoon pine nuts
1 tablespoon chopped fresh cilantro
1 teaspoon olive oil
12 large, stemmed spinach leaves
2 ounces soft, low-fat goat cheese
1 cup sliced crimini mushrooms
Olive oil cooking spray

1. Bring a small amount of water to a boil. Put the tomatoes in a small bowl, pour enough of the water over them to cover, and soak for 20 to 30 minutes. Drain.

2. Line a sheet pan with parchment paper, smooth-side down. Lay the chicken pieces between two sheets of plastic wrap. Using a meat mallet or the bottom of a small, heavy skillet, lightly pound them so that they're about ¼ inch thick. Transfer the pieces to the sheet pan.

3. Sprinkle the chicken with garlic, Herbamare, salt, and pepper. Refrigerate for at least 30 minutes, or until ready to cook, but not longer than overnight. (If you leave the chicken in the refrigerator overnight, do not soak the tomatoes until the next day.)

4. Preheat the oven to 400°F.

5. In a food processor fitted with the metal blade, process the sun-dried tomatoes, pine nuts, cilantro, and olive oil until pastelike. Spread this paste over the chicken.

6. Press 3 spinach leaves onto each piece of chicken and mound 2 teaspoons of goat cheese in the center of the leaves. Top with sliced mushrooms. Gently and tightly, roll the chicken away from you, starting at one of the short ends, to enclose the filling, spinach, and cheese.

7. Spray the top of each chicken roll with olive oil cooking spray. Season with more salt and pepper.

8. Arrange the rolls, seam-side down, in a shallow roasting pan. If the rolls seem too loose, secure them with toothpicks. Bake for about 20 minutes, until the chicken is cooked through and the filling is hot.

Per serving: 4 grams carbohydrates, 24 grams protein, 5 grams fat

Chicken Taco Salad

Whenever I have leftover chicken, I tend to make this taco salad. We especially like this in the summertime because it's so light and simple, but it's a hit any time of year. There is a lot of fat in the ingredients, but if you are at an acceptable weight, the fat won't interfere with your body's overall balance and you will stay in the Zone. You can cut back on the avocado and cheese to cut the fat. It's a snap to double or halve this recipe, and if you don't have quite enough chicken, make it anyway—the vegetables and cheese will fill out the taco. End the meal with fresh fruit.

Serves 4

¾ pound boneless, skinless chicken breasts*
1 1¼-ounce package taco seasoning (I use Bearitos)
1 cup shredded lettuce
8 crisp taco shells*
1 avocado, mashed
¼ cup low-fat shredded Monterey Jack cheese
½ cup salsa, or more, if you prefer
Chopped onion, tomato, and black olives, optional
Hot red pepper sauce, optional

1. Fill a deep skillet or sauté pan about halfway with water and bring it to a boil over high heat. Add the chicken, reduce the heat to medium so that the water simmers, and poach for about 30 minutes, adjusting the heat to maintain the simmer, until cooked through.

2. Remove the chicken pieces from the water and set them aside to cool. Using your fingers, shred the chicken meat and transfer it to a frying pan.

3. Add the taco seasoning and ⅔ cup water to the frying pan, mix well, and bring the contents to a simmer over medium-high heat. Cook for 8 to 10 minutes, adjusting the heat to maintain the simmer.

4. Divide the lettuce among the taco shells, and top with the hot chicken, avocado, salsa, and cheese. Garnish with chopped onion, tomato, and olives, if desired, and season with hot red pepper sauce, if desired.

Per serving: 13 grams carbohydrates, 28 grams protein, 20 grams fat

*You can poach the chicken several hours in advance, or even the day before, and keep it in the refrigerator until you're ready to make the tacos.

If you prefer to make this with a wheat or corn tortilla instead of a taco shell, lay the tortilla on a plate and top with the lettuce, chicken, avocado, and shredded cheese. (I like to use Bearitos blue corn shells.) Add your favorite salsa and other garnishes, such as onion, tomato, and olives. Season with a dash of hot sauce, and roll up the tortilla.

Zone Tip

If you think living in the Zone means never eating Mexican food, I have good news. The key is to balance your meal. For instance, if you choose a tortilla, do not have rice or beans. If you have a margarita, eat only vegetables and protein for your meal. The cooking process should use as little oil as possible. Fajitas are the best choice for a balanced meal, or have a burrito without rice and beans. If you're having a tostada, don't eat the shell or tortilla. Mexican salads with chicken or steak are Zone favorable.

Open-Face Avocado-Chicken Salad Sandwich

Avocadoes are terrific. They marry well with so many other ingredients, particularly with my favorite protein sources such as poultry and fish. Their smooth texture and natural moistness enhance a wide variety of dishes. I use mashed avocadoes to bind this chicken salad (and other salads in the book) much the way other cooks use mayonnaise. The monounsaturated fat in avocadoes is considered a favorable one for the Zone, and you can't argue with the potassium and folate, a water-soluble B vitamin, or the iron, magnesium, and vitamins A, C, E, and B_6 found in avocadoes. Make this with leftover chicken, if you have some, and if you are trying to keep your insulin levels low or are just getting into the Zone, eat this salad without the slice of bread.

Serves 1

½ cup shredded cooked chicken (about 3 ounces)
¼ cup mashed avocado (about ½ avocado)
1 stalk celery, finely chopped
1 tablespoon snipped fresh dill, optional
Hot sauce, optional
1 slice rye bread
Shredded lettuce
2 to 3 slices tomato
½ cup white or red seedless grapes

1. In a bowl, mix together the chicken, avocado, and celery. Add the dill, if using, and hot sauce to taste, if using, and stir well.

2. Toast the bread. Spoon the salad on the bread, and top with lettuce and tomato. Serve with grapes on the side.

Per serving: 37 grams carbohydrates, 21 grams protein, 9 grams fat

Zone Tip
When I poach chicken breasts, I usually poach a few extra, let them cool, and then wrap them well and freeze them for a month or so. This way, I know I have a ready-when-I-am protein source on hand. To make chicken broth at the same time, drop a few chopped carrots, onions, and ribs of celery into the poaching water. Strain and cool the liquid, and freeze it, too. Use this light, flavorful broth to moisten any number of dishes—it's essentially fat free.

Chicken Salad with Hot-and-Sweet Mustard Dressing

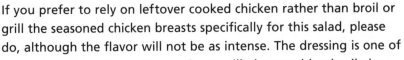

If you prefer to rely on leftover cooked chicken rather than broil or grill the seasoned chicken breasts specifically for this salad, please do, although the flavor will not be as intense. The dressing is one of my best, and you'll want to use it on grilled vegetables, broiled or poached fish, and even pork. Finish the meal with a cup of grapes.

Serves 2

Chicken salad
Vegetable oil cooking spray (if grilling)
2 whole skinless, boneless chicken breasts, each about 4 ounces
2 tablespoons grainy mustard
1 tablespoon fresh lemon juice
1 pound zucchini or summer squash, cut into thin strips
2 tablespoons chopped fresh flat-leaf parsley
2 tablespoons chopped scallion, white and green parts
2 teaspoons toasted sesame seeds

Mustard dressing
3 tablespoons rice vinegar
1½ tablespoons grainy mustard
1½ tablespoons brown rice syrup or honey
1½ tablespoons low-sodium tamari
1 tablespoon olive oil
1 tablespoon Splenda
2 garlic cloves
1½ teaspoons dry mustard
1½ teaspoons grated fresh ginger
⅛ teaspoon red pepper flakes
1 teaspoon toasted sesame oil

Garnish (optional)
Chopped pickled ginger or strips of pimiento

1. For the chicken, preheat the broiler, or prepare a charcoal or gas grill. If you're grilling, lightly coat the grill rack with vegetable oil cooking spray, and line it with heavy-duty aluminum foil; also coat the foil lightly with cooking spray. (This is not necessary if using the broiler.) The coals or heating elements are ready when they are medium-hot.

2. Lay the chicken between two sheets of plastic wrap. Using a meat mallet or the bottom of a small, heavy skillet, lightly pound the chicken breasts so that they are about ¼ inch thick. (You may ask the butcher to do this for you.)

3. In a small bowl, stir together the mustard and lemon juice.

4. Broil the chicken for 5 minutes on each side, brushing with the mustard mixture two or three times, or until cooked through. Cut the chicken into bite-size pieces and transfer to a mixing bowl.

5. Fill a large saucepan about halfway with water and bring it to a boil. Add the zucchini, return the water to a boil, and blanch for

about 1 minute, until the zucchini is slightly softened. Drain and cool. Add to the chicken.

6. Add the parsley, scallion, and sesame seeds to the bowl, and toss. Set aside to cool completely.

7. Meanwhile, make the dressing. In a blender, combine all the ingredients for the dressing and process until smooth.

8. Pour the dressing over the cooled salad and toss gently to mix. Serve at room temperature or chilled, garnished with ginger or pimiento, if using.

Per serving: 9 grams carbohydrates, 26 grams protein, 9 grams fat

Zone Tip
Exercise is important. Try to walk for at least 30 minutes a day, or engage in another aerobic exercise. Strength train several times a week. Exercise increases your metabolic rate and lowers excess blood glucose and insulin levels.

Smoked Turkey with Apples and Onions

Finally, I have successfully weaned my family and myself from the typical Thanksgiving turkey. By this, I mean we have abandoned the notion that turkey is *only* for the fall holiday and that the *only* way to cook it is in a boring moderate oven. The method described here is beyond delicious, but it does require tending. First, the turkey is prepped the night before and then refrigerated until ready to cook.

This means you should clear space in the refrigerator. While the turkey grills, the damp wood chips will impart light smokiness, and the cinnamon and cloves in the water pan will keep the bird pleasingly moist. But to achieve this perfection, you will have to replenish spent coals with live ones, add more water and wine to the pans, and scatter more chips over the coals. It's worth it, plus my family finds it fun to dash in and out on a chilly afternoon to tend to the magnificent bird.

Serves 14

1 14-pound turkey
1 head garlic, cloves separated
4 to 5 sprigs fresh rosemary
2 large yellow onions, 1 halved and 1 sliced
1 firm tart apple, halved
Herbamare
Sea salt and freshly ground pepper
1 bottle (75 ml) white wine or dry vermouth
1 cup hardwood chips, such as oak, apple, or mesquite
2 cinnamon sticks
4 cloves

1. Rinse the turkey thoroughly inside and out in cold water, drain, pat dry with paper towels, and set breast-side up on a rack in a roasting pan.

2. In a small food processor or with a sharp knife, chop the garlic cloves. Spread about half of the chopped garlic in the cavity of the turkey and reserve the rest.

3. Work your fingers between the skin and breast meat to loosen the skin. Insert the rosemary and about half of the remaining chopped garlic under the loosened skin, and smooth in place.

4. Put the onion halves and apple halves in the cavity. (If they don't all fit, slice whatever's left over and scatter it over the turkey.) Season the turkey heavily, inside and out, with Herbamare, salt, and pepper.

5. Scatter the onion slices and the rest of the chopped garlic over and around the turkey. Pour the wine over the turkey and inside the cavity. Cover with foil and refrigerate overnight.

6. Soak the hardwood chips in water overnight or for at least 1 hour.

7. Remove the turkey from the refrigerator, remove the foil, and let it sit at room temperature for about 30 minutes to take off the chill. This promotes even cooking.

8. Prepare a large, covered charcoal or gas grill by arranging the coals or heating elements around the perimeter of the grill. Set a small metal or aluminum pan in the center, fill it with 3 inches of water, and add the cinnamon sticks and cloves.

9. Light the coals, and when they're covered with a layer of gray ash and smoldering red beneath the ash, scatter half of the wood chips over them. The chips will begin to smoke.

10. Put the turkey still in the roasting pan directly over the pan of water. Cover the grill and roast for 12 to 20 minutes per pound, depending on the weather. Very cold weather (35°F or lower) requires more time. For a 14-pound turkey, allow about 3 hours and 20 minutes in warm weather and about 4 hours in very cold weather.

11. Keep the fire moderately cool, which means a thermometer inserted in the vent of the grill should register about 325°F. Add more coals as necessary (you can start them in a charcoal chimney and keep them on hand), and add more wine or water to the pan as it evaporates. Scatter the remaining chips over the coals about halfway through roasting. Turn the turkey once during cooking.

When the initial liquid evaporates, add more wine or water to the roasting pan. Otherwise, keep the grill covered the whole time.

12. The turkey is done when you puncture it and its juices run clear, a leg moves easily around in its joint, and a meat thermometer registers 170°F when inserted in the breast meat (do not touch the bone) or 180°F in the dark meat.

13. Let the turkey rest for about 15 minutes. Remove the onion and apple halves from the cavity and discard. Slice the turkey and serve; smoked turkey may have a pinkish tinge near the bone, which is normal.

Per serving: 0 grams carbohydrates, 28 grams protein, 0 grams fat

Variation

Smoked Turkey Breast with Southwestern Seasoning and Salsa:
When you smoke the turkey breast, omit the garlic, rosemary, onion, and apple. Instead, rub the turkey cavity and skin with several tablespoons of chili powder, as well as salt, pepper, and Herbamare. Pour the wine over the turkey, let it sit overnight in the refrigerator, and proceed as directed in the recipe. This method works very well with a turkey breast, too. Serve the turkey with Southwestern Salsa, page 249.

Roasted Teriyaki Turkey Breast

This easy roasted turkey breast is a perfect example of a meal that tastes good year-round and proves the point that turkey is most certainly not just for the fourth Thursday in November. Plus, leftovers can be used for any of the chicken salads in this book, not to mention recipes that call for cooked turkey. And a slice of white-meat turkey is a wonderful Zone-friendly protein snack. Serve this with spinach, fruit salad, and a glass of white or red wine.

Serves 8

1 2-pound boneless turkey breast
¾ cup low-sodium tamari or soy sauce
½ cup fresh lemon juice
½ cup low-sodium chicken broth
¼ cup sherry
2 garlic cloves, minced
1¼ teaspoons ground ginger

1. Put the turkey breast in a shallow glass baking dish or similar nonreactive dish.

2. In a small bowl, stir together the tamari, lemon juice, chicken broth, sherry, garlic, and ginger. Pour or spoon the mixture over the turkey breast, and turn to coat as well as you can. Cover and refrigerate for at least 6 hours and up to 12 hours.

3. Preheat the oven to 325°F.

4. Transfer the turkey to a roasting pan. Reserve the marinade for basting.

5. Roast for 50 to 60 minutes, or until a meat thermometer registers 170°F. Baste often with the marinade during the first 15 minutes of cooking.

Per serving: 1.5 grams carbohydrates, 24 grams protein, 0 grams fat

Sautéed Turkey Breast with Mushrooms and Garlic

Rather than wheat flour, I turn to almond flour to coat turkey slices for quick cooking in a lovely and classic mixture of olive oil and lemon juice. The almonds add fat grams to this recipe, but because fat does not raise insulin levels or otherwise affect hormones, you stay in the Zone. Serve this with steamed broccoli and carrots, which mingle nicely with the sautéed mushrooms. For dessert? Try sliced pineapple or another fruit.

Serves 2

½ pound boneless turkey breast, 6 to 8 slices
¼ cup almond flour*
Olive oil cooking spray
1 tablespoon olive oil
Juice of ½ lemon
Herbamare
Freshly ground black pepper
10 white or crimini mushrooms, thinly sliced
2 garlic cloves, minced
½ cup dry white wine or dry vermouth

1. Score the edges of the turkey slices two to four times to prevent curling.

2. Spread the almond flour on a plate and dredge the turkey slices with it to coat both sides lightly.

3. Coat a large nonstick skillet with olive oil cooking spray. Put ½ tablespoon of the olive oil and half of the lemon juice in the pan, and heat over medium-high heat until the oil easily coats the bottom of the pan. Add the turkey slices, season with Herbamare and

pepper, and sauté for about 4 minutes on each side, until lightly browned and cooked through. Remove the slices as they are browned and arrange them on a serving platter. Add the remaining olive oil and lemon juice to the skillet as needed.

4. Add the mushrooms and garlic to the skillet, and sauté for about 2 minutes. Add the wine, and bring the contents to a boil over high heat, scraping up the browned pieces stuck to the bottom of the skillet with a wooden spoon. Reduce the heat to medium and simmer for about 5 minutes, until the sauce flavors are blended.

5. Pour the sauce over the turkey slices and serve.

Per serving: 2 grams carbohydrates, 24 grams protein, 12 grams fat

*Almond flour is easy to make in a blender or food processor. For the ¼ cup needed here, you will need about an ounce of slivered almonds—although, I suggest you grind a little more to be on the safe side. Almond flour is also sold in specialty stores and natural food markets. Use it within a week of grinding or buying, as it does not keep well.

Turkey-Apple Quesadillas

Quesadillas are classic snacks, easy lunches, or even quick suppers, and this recipe is about as good as they get. You can buy smoked turkey at the deli, or use leftover Smoked Turkey with Apples and Onions, page 187. The mustard perks up the flavor, and the apple slices add interest and texture. I think you'll like this!

Serves 2

Hot-and-sweet or your favorite store-bought mustard
2 6-inch corn or flour tortillas
4 ounces sliced smoked turkey
1 firm tart apple, peeled and thinly sliced
2 ounces low-fat mozzarella, low-fat cheddar, or soy cheese, thinly
   sliced
Olive oil cooking spray

1. Spread mustard on one side of each tortilla.

2. Lay the turkey, apple, and cheese on one of the tortillas. Top with
the other tortilla, mustard-side down, to form a "sandwich."

3. Spray a nonstick skillet or griddle with olive oil cooking spray and
heat over medium heat. Place the quesadilla in the pan and cook for
2 to 3 minutes, turning once with a wide spatula, until the cheese
melts and the tortillas are lightly browned. Cut in half and serve.

Per serving: 11 grams carbohydrates, 22 grams protein, 3.6 grams fat

Zone Tip

The next time you're buying cheese, try soy cheese. Dairy free,
cholesterol free, low in fat and calories, and yet high in protein,
calcium, vitamins, and minerals, it's hard to knock. Soy cheese
melts like dairy cheese and tastes good, too. It's completely
natural and also kosher!

Tex-Mex Turkey Tortillas

Wraps—sandwich fillings folded in tortillas or similar flatbreads—are
endlessly versatile and exceedingly popular. This is one of my

favorites because it's true to the flavors that naturally ally with tortillas: black beans, cilantro, chili powder, cumin, and avocado. If you prefer to forgo the tortilla and eat this as a salad, toss the ingredients with lettuce and add another quarter cup of black beans. The nutritional values will remain the same.

Serves 4

4 cups coarsely chopped or shredded cooked turkey
½ cup cooked or canned and drained black beans
¼ cup chopped pimiento
¼ cup chopped fresh cilantro
1 ounce pitted, canned black olives, sliced
¼ cup olive oil
2 tablespoons apple cider vinegar
2 teaspoons chili powder
⅛ teaspoon ground cumin
Sea salt or Herbamare
Freshly ground pepper
4 6-inch whole wheat tortillas
About 2 cups shredded lettuce
½ red onion, sliced
1 ripe avocado, sliced

1. In a bowl, mix together the turkey, black beans, pimiento, cilantro, and olives.

2. In another bowl, whisk together the olive oil, vinegar, chili powder, and cumin. Season to taste with salt and pepper. Pour over the turkey mixture and toss to combine. Set aside for 10 to 15 minutes for the flavors to develop.

3. Divide the turkey salad among the tortillas, laying it down the center of each one. Top with lettuce, onion, and avocado, taking care not to overfill them. Roll the tortillas and serve.

Per serving: 11 grams carbohydrates, 24 grams protein, 19 grams fat

Sweet-and-Sour Turkey Meatballs

A winner on a chilly afternoon or evening! The ground turkey, flavored with garlic and ginger and moistened with egg whites, makes juicy meatballs that taste delectable with the fruity sauce. This reheats really well, so you can make it ahead of time, if that is easier for you. Serve it with Lentil and Spinach Casserole, page 242, and Poached Pears, page 260.

Serves 6

Meatballs
1 pound ground turkey breast
⅓ cup drained and chopped canned water chestnuts
2 egg whites
2 garlic cloves, minced
2 slices fresh ginger, chopped (about 2 teaspoons)
1 tablespoon low-sodium soy sauce
1 tablespoon dry sherry
2 teaspoons cornstarch
½ teaspoon sea salt or Herbamare
2 teaspoons olive oil

Sauce
3 tablespoons unsweetened pineapple juice
1 tablespoon low-sodium soy sauce
2 teaspoons apple cider vinegar
1½ teaspoons ketchup
1 garlic clove, minced
1 slice fresh ginger, chopped (about 1 teaspoon)
Toasted sesame oil

1. Preheat the oven to 350°F.

2. To make the meatballs, in a mixing bowl, combine the turkey, water chestnuts, egg whites, garlic, ginger, soy sauce, sherry,

cornstarch, and salt. Mix well and form into balls about the size of Ping-Pong or golf balls.

3. In a large nonstick skillet, heat the olive oil over medium-high heat. When the oil easily coats the pan, add the meatballs and cook for 7 to 10 minutes, turning several times, until evenly browned. Transfer the meatballs to a shallow baking dish and bake for about 10 minutes.

4. Meanwhile, make the sauce. In a mixing bowl, stir together the pineapple juice, soy sauce, vinegar, ketchup, garlic, and ginger. Add a few drops of sesame oil to taste.

5. Pull the baking dish from the oven and pour the sauce over the meatballs. Toss to coat. Return the meatballs to the oven and bake for 10 minutes longer, or until the meat is cooked through and the sauce is hot.

Per serving: 3 grams carbohydrates, 22 grams protein, 1.5 grams fat

Asian Turkey Burgers

If you have a hankering for burgers on the grill, you'll want to sink your teeth into these. You won't even miss the buns! Grill some pineapple, bell pepper, and onion rings alongside the burgers for an outstanding Zone-friendly summer meal. When you buy ground turkey, look for ground turkey breast, which is leaner and milder tasting than other ground turkey. The meat tends toward dryness, which is why I almost always combine it with a little moisture, such as the soy sauce and oil here.

Serves 4

Vegetable oil cooking spray (if grilling)
1 pound ground turkey breast
2 tablespoons low-sodium soy sauce
1½ tablespoons thinly sliced scallions (1 to 2 scallions), white and
    green parts
1 tablespoon toasted sesame oil
¼ teaspoon crushed dried red pepper flakes
2 garlic cloves, minced
2 tablespoons chopped fresh cilantro
4 cups torn red leaf or romaine lettuce

1. Preheat the broiler, or prepare a charcoal or gas grill. If grilling,
lightly coat the grill rack with vegetable oil cooking spray. The coals
or heating elements are ready when they are medium-hot.

2. In a mixing bowl, combine the turkey, 1½ tablespoons of the soy
sauce, scallions, sesame oil, pepper flakes, garlic, and cilantro. Shape
into four patties, each about 1 inch thick. Brush each patty with the
remaining ½ tablespoon soy sauce.

3. Broil the burgers, or grill on medium heat, for about 10 minutes,
turning once, until well browned, firm, and cooked through. Do not
overcook.

4. Spread the lettuce on a serving platter and top with the burgers.
Add more soy sauce or teriyaki sauce, if desired, and serve.

Per serving: 0 grams carbohydrates, 24 grams protein, 3.5 grams fat

Veal Scaloppine Marsala

There's nothing wrong with eating meat as long as you choose lean cuts and don't eat it often. Veal is a good protein choice. Ask the butcher to pound the cutlets very thin, called scaloppine, or do it yourself, as explained below. It's no sweat: you just enclose them in wax paper or cellophane and give them a few bangs with a meat mallet—or even a skillet. This dish, made as it is with mushrooms and marsala wine, is a classic and one whose flavors never fail to please. It's even more pleasing when paired with a mix of stir-fried or sautéed red bell peppers, pea pods, carrots, onions, and broccoli. Add a small serving of wild rice and a glass of red wine and you have a great meal!

Serves 4

1 pound veal cutlets
¼ cup grated low-fat Parmesan or soy Parmesan cheese
2 teaspoons olive oil
2 garlic cloves, minced
1 cup sliced mushrooms
Herbamare
Dash of cayenne
¼ cup low-sodium beef broth
¼ cup marsala or sherry

1. Put the veal cutlets between two sheets of wax paper or plastic wrap. Using a meat mallet or the bottom of a small, heavy skillet, gently flatten them until they're about ⅜ inch thick. Cut the meat into strips about 2 inches wide, and sprinkle both sides with Parmesan.

2. In a large nonstick skillet, heat 1 teaspoon of the olive oil over medium-high heat. When the oil easily coats the pan, add the veal

and sauté for about 5 minutes, until lightly browned on both sides and cooked through. Transfer to a warm platter.

3. Put the remaining teaspoon of olive oil in the skillet, add the garlic, and sauté for about 1 minute, until it's softened but not colored. Add the mushrooms, and season to taste with Herbamare and cayenne. Sauté for 5 to 7 minutes longer, or until the mushrooms soften. Spoon the mushrooms over the veal.

4. Add the beef broth to the pan, and use a wooden spoon to scrape the brown bits stuck to the bottom and mix them into the broth. Cook over medium-high heat until the broth simmers. Add the marsala and raise the heat to high. When the liquid comes to a boil, reduce the heat and simmer the sauce for about 3 minutes, until the flavors blend. Pour the sauce over the veal and mushrooms, and serve.

Per serving: 2 grams carbohydrates, 28 grams protein, 3 grams fat (0.5 gram fat with soy cheese)

Zone Tip

The right knives are essential to cooking. Invest in an 8-inch chef's knife, a 3½-inch paring knife, and a good-quality serrated knife. Keep them sharp (sharp knives are safe knives), and never put them in the dishwasher. Their edges will dull as they knock against the other utensils, and the very hot water is not good for wooden handles.

Marinated Lamb Kabobs

Chunks of tender lamb, cut from the leg, make terrific kabobs. In fact, lamb is the meat of choice for classic shish kebab. For this recipe, I marinate the meat and the vegetables separately and then thread them on skewers for a quick stint over the hot fire. An excellent summertime, in-the-Zone feast! I love to serve this with grilled fruit kabobs.

Serves 8

2 pounds lamb, cut from the leg, trimmed of any fat
12 portobello mushrooms, quartered
2½ pounds green bell peppers (7 to 8 peppers), cut into 2-inch strips
3 large sweet onions, such as Vidalia or Walla Walla, quartered
½ pound cherry tomatoes
1½ cups pineapple juice
½ cup low-sodium tamari or soy sauce
¼ cup dry red wine
¼ cup chopped fresh mint
3 tablespoons finely chopped garlic
1 teaspoon ground black pepper
Vegetable oil cooking spray

1. Cut the lamb into 1½-inch cubes. Put the cubes in a rigid plastic container or plastic zip bag.

2. Put the mushrooms, bell peppers, onions, and tomatoes in another plastic container or plastic bag.

3. In a small bowl, mix together the pineapple juice, tamari, wine, mint, garlic, and black pepper. Pour half of the marinade over the meat and the other half over the vegetables. Seal the containers and refrigerate both for at least 3 hours and up to 12 hours, turning occasionally.

4. Soak eight wooden skewers in cold water for at least 1 hour, or use metal skewers.

5. Prepare a charcoal or gas grill. Lightly coat the grill rack with vegetable oil cooking spray. The coals or heating elements are ready when they are medium-hot.

6. Thread the lamb and vegetables on the skewers, alternating the meat with a different vegetable.

7. Grill for about 10 minutes, turning the skewers several times, until the meat is medium-rare.

Per serving: 12 grams carbohydrates, 28 grams protein, 3 grams fat

Grilled Lemon-Basil Pork Chops

As you can quickly tell from the recipes in this book, I pretty much stay away from meat. I favor chicken, turkey, and fish but every now and then serve meat. My son jumps for joy when I dish up these pork chops. And why not? When the pork is lightly coated with a homemade herb-lemon mix, it develops a tantalizing crust on the grill, and it tastes great with the grilled red peppers. Substitute lamb or veal chops if you prefer, being sure to trim all visible fat. Serve this with salad, Chick-Peas with Broccoli Rabe, page 245, and The Best Applesauce, page 259.

Serves 4

Vegetable oil cooking spray
3 tablespoons finely chopped fresh basil
3 tablespoons finely chopped fresh parsley

1 garlic clove, crushed
1 teaspoon grated lemon zest
2 red bell peppers, halved
2 teaspoons olive oil
4 rib or loin pork chops, each about 1 inch thick
Sea salt and freshly ground black pepper

1. Prepare a charcoal or gas grill. Lightly coat the grill rack with vegetable oil cooking spray. The coals or heating elements are ready when they are medium-hot.

2. In a small bowl, mix together the basil, parsley, garlic, and lemon zest. Set 1 tablespoon of the seasoning mix aside.

3. Brush the bell peppers with the olive oil. Coat the pork chops and the peppers with the seasoning mix, pressing it into the meat on both sides.

4. Grill the chops and peppers for 12 to 14 minutes, turning both several times, until the meat is cooked through and the peppers are tender.

5. Sprinkle the reserved tablespoon of seasoning on the chops, and add salt and black pepper to taste. Cut each pepper half into three pieces. Serve the peppers alongside the pork chops.

Per serving: 2.5 grams carbohydrates, 28 grams protein, 3 grams fat

Tofu, Tempeh, and Other Vegetarian Main Courses

Marinated Tofu

For the best-tasting tofu, make sure to extract as much water as you can from the block. First, I press it by hand, and then I wrap it in absorbent cloth and weigh it down with cans or other heavy objects. After it's marinated, how you prepare it determines how much of the marinade stays with the tofu. If you bake it, as I do here, more of the absorbed marinade will remain in the finished dish than if you grill it. But the flavors will be different, too. This is a pretty classic tofu preparation and makes a satisfying main course. Serve with some brown rice and the Oven-Roasted Orange Vegetables on page 244.

Serves 2

1 1-pound block extra-firm tofu*
¼ cup orange juice
⅓ cup low-sodium tamari or soy sauce
2 tablespoons sake*
2 tablespoons mirin*
1 teaspoon grated fresh ginger
2 teaspoons sesame seeds
¼ teaspoon dried oregano
2 teaspoons grated orange zest
Cayenne

1. Lift the block of tofu from the package and gently press it between your fingers to remove any excess water. Wrap the tofu in a double thickness of cheesecloth or a clean kitchen towel, set it on a plate, and set another plate on top of it. Place heavy cans or other weights on the top plate to compress the tofu for 15 minutes.

2. In a nonreactive mixing bowl, stir together the orange juice, tamari, sake, mirin, ginger, sesame seeds, oregano, and orange zest. Season to taste with cayenne.

3. Unwrap the tofu and cut it horizontally into two slabs. Cut each slab vertically into thirds, so that you end up with six slices. Lay the tofu slices in a shallow glass, ceramic, or other nonreactive dish, pour the marinade over them, and turn them a few times to coat. Set aside for 1 hour at room temperature (if it's a hot summer day—over 75° or 80°F—refrigerate the tofu).

4. Preheat the oven to 350°F.

5. Lift the tofu from the marinade and transfer it to a shallow baking dish. Bake for about 30 minutes, turning once, until the tofu is golden to dark brown.

6. Serve the tofu warm or at room temperature.

Per serving: 13 grams carbohydrates, 27 grams protein, 1 gram fat

*The nutritional values of tofu vary from one brand to another, so check the labels to be sure you are getting the most protein. I'm fond of Nasoya brand. Both firm and extra-firm tofu have 7 grams of protein per 3-ounce serving.

Both sake and mirin, which is sweeter, are rice wines. While both have low alcohol contents, sake is more alcoholic, with levels as high as 16 percent. Sake is sold in liquor stores, but because mirin has such a low alcohol content, it's sold in the Asian section of many supermarkets and natural food stores.

Marinated Nigari Tofu

This is similar to the preceding recipe, but the marinade is a little sweeter. Also like the preceding recipe, it's terrific as a main course, particularly if you are experimenting with eating more tofu. Nigari is

the firmest type of tofu. You'll like this a lot, I promise, especially if you serve it with the Lentil and Spinach Casserole, page 242, and some sliced fresh pineapple for dessert.

Serves 2

1 1-pound block extra-firm tofu
2 garlic cloves, minced
¼ teaspoon toasted sesame oil
2 tablespoons low-sodium tamari
1 tablespoon mirin (see note on page 207)
1 tablespoon fresh lemon juice
1 to 2 teaspoons brown rice syrup or honey
Crushed red pepper flakes

1. Lift the block of tofu from the package and gently press it between your fingers to remove any excess water. Wrap the tofu in a double thickness of cheesecloth or a clean kitchen towel, set it on a plate, and set another plate on top of it. Place heavy cans or other weights on the top plate to compress the tofu for 15 minutes.

2. In a shallow glass, ceramic, or other nonreactive dish, stir together the garlic, sesame oil, tamari, mirin, and lemon juice. Add 1 teaspoon of rice syrup, taste, and add more if needed. Season to taste with red pepper flakes.

3. Unwrap the tofu and cut it horizontally into two slabs. Cut each slab vertically into thirds, so that you end up with six slices. Lay the tofu slices in the dish with the marinade, and turn them a few times to coat. Set aside for 1 hour at room temperature, or for up to 12 hours in the refrigerator; turn the slices every 30 minutes, tilting the dish periodically, so that the marinade penetrates the tofu.

4. Preheat the oven to 350°F.

5. Lift the tofu from the marinade and transfer it to a shallow baking dish. Bake for about 30 minutes, turning once, until the tofu is golden to dark brown.

6. Serve the tofu warm, at room temperature, or chilled.

Per serving: 8 grams carbohydrates, 26 grams protein, 1 gram fat

Italian-Flavored Tofu Sausage with Vegetables

Italian-style vegetarian sausages, made by a company called Lightlife, are sold in the refrigerator section of supermarkets alongside the tofu. They are a real find—only 3 grams of fat per link and chock-full of Italian flavor—and taste delicious in this mix of peppers, mushrooms, and tomatoes. I suggest you serve this with ⅓ cup cooked whole wheat pasta.

Serves 2

6 sun-dried tomatoes
2 teaspoons olive oil
8 links old-world Italian-flavored tofu sausage
¼ cup dry vermouth
1 zucchini, cut into matchsticks
1 garlic clove, minced
½ cup sliced white or crimini mushrooms
½ red bell pepper, diced
½ yellow bell pepper, diced
Olive oil cooking spray
½ teaspoon crushed dried basil, or 1 tablespoon chopped fresh basil
Crushed red pepper flakes
Grated soy Parmesan cheese, optional

1. In a small bowl, soak the sun-dried tomatoes in enough water to cover them for at least 20 minutes. Drain, reserve the soaking water, and chop the tomatoes. Set both aside.

2. In a large nonstick frying pan, heat the olive oil over medium-high heat. When the oil easily coats the pan, add the tofu links and cook for about 10 minutes, mashing with a fork until they crumble and are lightly browned. During the cooking, when the pan becomes dry, add the vermouth a little at a time. (It's nearly impossible to "overcook" the links, and they taste better when cooked for the full 10 minutes or even a few minutes longer, but take care not to burn them.)

3. Add the zucchini, garlic, mushrooms, and red and yellow bell peppers to the skillet, spray with a little olive oil cooking spray, and sauté for about 7 minutes, until the peppers are soft.

4. Add the chopped tomatoes and enough of their soaking water to moisten the sausage. Stir in the basil and then season to taste with red pepper flakes.

5. Serve hot, garnished with soy Parmesan, if desired.

Per serving: 14 grams carbohydrates, 21 grams protein, 7 grams fat

Nutty Vegetables with Tofu

I make this quick-and-easy, colorful tofu-vegetable salad with the grilled tofu sold in the refrigerator case of most supermarkets and natural food markets. Of course, you could use one of the baked tofu recipes on pages 206 and 207, instead. I really like this with

sugar snap peas, although pea pods would work well, too. To prepare the sugar snaps, break off the tips and drag the string along the pod to remove it; then trim the other side. This is equally suitable as a light main course, a snack, or lunch. I keep it in the refrigerator for up to 4 days.

Serves 2

½ pound fresh sugar snap peas, strings removed, sliced diagonally into 2 or 3 pieces
2 carrots, slivered
1 red bell pepper, diced
1 pound extra-firm grilled tofu or extra-firm tofu
¼ cup chopped scallion
1½ tablespoons creamy peanut butter
2 tablespoons chopped fresh cilantro
1 tablespoon rice vinegar
2 teaspoons water
2 teaspoons low-sodium soy sauce
½ teaspoon chili-garlic sauce
Pinch of sea salt or Herbamare

1. Bring a pot of water to a boil over high heat. Add the sugar snap peas and carrots, and blanch them in the boiling water for 1 minute. Drain the vegetables and refresh them under cool running water. Put them in a large bowl, add the bell pepper, and set aside.

2. Lift the block of tofu from the package and set it on a plate. Let any excess moisture drain off. Transfer to a cutting board and cut it horizontally into two slabs, and then cut the slabs vertically into thirds, so that you end up with six slices. Put the tofu slices in the bowl with the vegetables.

3. In a nonreactive bowl, whisk together the scallion, peanut butter, cilantro, vinegar, water, soy sauce, and garlic sauce. Season to taste with salt.

4. Pour or spoon the peanut dressing over the vegetables and tofu, and toss gently to mix. Serve.

Per serving: 16 grams carbohydrates, 27 grams protein, 6 grams fat

Tempeh-Vegetable Salad

If you're a vegetarian, this recipe is for you—and even if you are not strictly vegetarian but are partial to nonmeat dishes, this is for you. Tempeh, a protein-rich soy product, is an excellent choice for people trying to work more soy into their diets. As high in protein as beef and chicken, it can be steamed, as in this preparation, baked, grilled, or stir-fried. Made from fermented soybeans, tempeh is rich in soy isoflavones and, as such, protects against some cancers. Sample this salad when you might otherwise have tuna or chicken salad and serve it with half a whole wheat pita and half an apple. You won't be disappointed, and you will be happily eating in the Zone.

Serves 2

Salad
1 8-ounce package soy tempeh
1 small carrot, grated
1 rib celery, finely chopped
½ yellow onion, finely minced
2 teaspoons snipped fresh dill or chopped fresh tarragon
1 tablespoon finely minced flat-leaf parsley

Dressing
½ cup Nayonaise (soy mayonnaise) or light mayonnaise
1 tablespoon brown rice vinegar
1 teaspoon Dijon mustard

Juice of ½ lemon
Freshly ground white pepper
Dash of cayenne

1. To cook the tempeh, bring a large pan only partially filled with
water to a boil. Put the tempeh in the basket of a steamer or in a
vegetable steaming basket, cover tightly, and steam over the boiling
water at medium-high for 30 minutes.

2. Transfer the tempeh to a bowl and mash it with a fork until well
crumbled, about the texture of crumbly cheese. (If the tempeh cools
before you mash it, it's fine.) Add the carrot, celery, onion, dill, and
parsley, and toss well.

3. For the dressing, in a small bowl, stir together the Nayonaise,
vinegar, mustard, and lemon juice. Season to taste with white pepper
and cayenne.

4. Spoon the dressing over the tempeh and vegetables, and toss
gently to mix. Serve at room temperature or chilled. The salad will
keep, covered and refrigerated, for up to 4 days.

Per serving: 16 grams carbohydrates, 22 grams protein, 12 grams fat

Chili-in-the-Zone

For many families, chili is a staple, and home cooks tend to have
their own, very personal recipes. This is mine, and like the majority
of chili recipes, it has a long list of ingredients that essentially are all
dumped into one pot and cooked. Easy! My chili sits firmly in the
Zone. It's soy based, with plenty of vegetables and lots of great

flavor. I like mild chili powder, such as Chimayo Style Chile Powder, which I buy online from the Santa Fe School of Cooking. But use your favorite, and if you like more heat, go for a hotter type.

Serves 4

1 tablespoon olive oil
¼ to ½ cup dry white wine or dry vermouth
1 large yellow onion, chopped
2 garlic cloves, minced
4 cups soy crumbles* (2 14-ounce packages)
1 pound extra-firm tofu, squeezed dry and cubed
2 tablespoons chili powder
½ teaspoon dried basil
½ teaspoon dried oregano
½ teaspoon cumin
2 cups finely chopped zucchini
1 cup finely chopped carrot
2 cups cooked kidney beans plus ½ cup of the cooking water, or
    2 cups canned, undrained
2 28-ounce cans tomatoes, drained and coarsely chopped
Herbamare or sea salt

Garnish
Chopped onion
Chopped tomato
Torn lettuce
Chopped green bell pepper
4 ounces low-fat Monterey Jack cheese, grated

1. In a large pot, heat the olive oil over medium-high heat until it slides over the bottom. Add ¼ cup wine, the onion, and the garlic, and sauté for 4 to 5 minutes, or until the onion is translucent. Add the soy crumbles and cubed tofu and stir with a wooden spoon, crumbling the soy even further and mixing it with the onion and garlic. If the pot gets dry, add a little more wine.

2. Reduce the heat to low, add the chili powder, basil, oregano, and cumin, and stir well. Stir in the zucchini and carrot, and cook for about 1 minute, stirring occasionally. Stir in the kidney beans and their liquid and the tomatoes.

3. Raise the heat to high until the chili comes to a boil. Reduce the heat to medium, and simmer for 30 to 45 minutes, adjusting the heat to maintain the simmer, until thick. Season to taste with Herbamare.

4. Serve the chili with the garnishes passed on the side.

Per serving: 29 grams carbohydrates, 21 grams protein, 1.5 grams fat

*I use Gimme Lean brand soy crumbles. I also like Morning Star brand. You will find these and other brands in natural food stores and many supermarkets. Choose the one you like best.

Zone Tip
The fiber in legumes such as beans and lentils is healthful, but it may inhibit the body's ability to absorb the protein in the legumes. So, eat legumes mainly for fiber and carbohydrates, and get most of your protein elsewhere.

Zucchini Lasagna

If you think lasagna has to be made with pasta, think again! My vegetarian lasagna made with slices of zucchini dividing the layers not only features the traditional rich tomato sauce mingled with melting, oozing cheese but also is a creative way to use the zucchini that overtakes our gardens at the end of the summer. And when homegrown isn't happening, you can always get zucchini in the markets. Serve this with a large green salad with carrots to raise the carbohydrate levels a little, add a glass of earthy Italian red wine, and then finish this Zone-friendly meal with the Chocolate-Covered Strawberries on page 263.

Serves 4

2 cups store-bought marinara sauce*
4 large zucchini, sliced ½ inch thick
½ pound skim-milk ricotta cheese
½ yellow onion, sliced
4 ounces white mushrooms, sliced
½ tablespoon ground dried oregano, or 2 tablespoons fresh
½ tablespoon dried basil, or 2 tablespoons fresh
Herbamare
½ pound low-fat mozzarella or soy mozzarella cheese, sliced
¼ cup grated low-fat Parmesan or soy Parmesan cheese
Toasted sunflower seeds, optional

1. Preheat the oven to 350°F.

2. Spread half of the marinara sauce in an 8-inch square baking dish. Top with half of the zucchini slices and then with layers of half each of the ricotta, onion, and mushrooms. Sprinkle with half of the oregano and basil, and season to taste with Herbamare. Top with a layer of half of the mozzarella.

3. Cover with the remaining cup of marinara sauce and repeat the layering process (if desired, set aside a few zucchini slices or mushrooms to dot the top), ending with the mozzarella. Sprinkle with the Parmesan, and garnish with sunflower seeds, if using, and a few slices of zucchini or mushrooms, if desired.

4. Bake for about 45 minutes, until the zucchini is cooked through but not mushy.

Per serving: 11 grams carbohydrates, 29 grams protein, 14 grams fat (12 grams fat with soy cheese)

*I like Muir Glen Chunky Tomato & Herb Pasta Sauce, but use your favorite brand. If you don't have a favorite, check the labels and buy the sauce with the fewest carbohydrates.

Sweet-and-Sour Cabbage

My aunt Florence passed down a recipe similar to this that our family had loved over the years, and I modified it to fit into my life in the Zone. It's just as good as the original, with all the old-fashioned comfort of stuffed cabbage leaves gently baked in a sweet-and-sour tomato sauce. At first read, it may seem more involved than many of my other recipes, but I always have fun wrapping the cabbage leaves into little packages, and the outcome is well worth the modest effort. To make this a Zone-favorable meal, add a green salad and, for dessert, baked peaches or apples with a scattering of slivered almonds.

Serves 4

8 large cabbage leaves, tough center ribs removed
4 cups soy crumbles, or 1 pound ground turkey breast
¼ cup egg substitute, or 2 eggs, beaten
½ tart apple, peeled and coarsely grated
2 tablespoons grated yellow onion
1 garlic clove, minced
Herbamare and freshly ground pepper
1 14-ounce can diced tomatoes, with juice
Juice of 1 lemon
2 tablespoons Splenda, or more if needed

1. Preheat the oven to 350°F. Boil about 2 quarts of water.

2. Lay the cabbage leaves in a shallow dish, and pour the boiling water over them. Let them soak for 15 minutes to soften. Drain.

3. Meanwhile, in a bowl, mix the soy crumbles with the egg substitute, apple, onion, garlic, and a light sprinkling of Herbamare and pepper. Form the mixture into eight rounded patties.

4. Put a patty on the end of each cabbage leaf and roll into a neat package. Transfer the cabbage rolls, seam-side down, to a 9″×13″ shallow baking dish large enough to hold them snugly in a single layer. Pour the tomatoes, their juices, and about a cup of water over the cabbage rolls, and bake, covered, for about 1 hour, until the tomato sauce is thickened and the cabbage rolls are soft and cooked through.

5. In a small bowl, stir together the lemon juice and 2 tablespoons of Splenda. Pull the baking dish from the oven, and pour the juice mixture evenly over the cabbage rolls. Return the dish to the oven and bake uncovered for about 10 minutes longer, until lightly browned. Taste and add more Splenda if it's not sweet enough.

Per serving: 15 grams carbohydrates, 25 grams protein, 0 grams fat

Black Bean and Soy Skillet Jumble

Skillet meals are dandy kitchen fare. Serve them straight from the pan, with everyone sitting around the kitchen table. When I was reviewing this recipe to include in the book, I couldn't decide if the main ingredient should be soy crumbles or turkey. Or perhaps I

should go with chopped soy hot dogs, cubed firm tofu, or Italian-style vegetarian sausage? All are scrumptious. In the end, I went with soy crumbles because they make it such a good vegetarian main course. But use any of the above for a very good Zone meal.

Serves 2

1 tablespoon olive oil
1 yellow onion, chopped
4 garlic cloves, minced
2 cups soy crumbles, or ½ pound ground white-meat turkey
1 teaspoon dried basil
1 teaspoon dried oregano
¾ teaspoon ground coriander
½ teaspoon cumin
½ teaspoon Herbamare or sea salt
⅛ teaspoon cayenne
⅛ teaspoon black pepper
1 15-ounce can black beans, drained
1 14-ounce can diced tomatoes, drained

1. In a large nonstick frying pan, heat the olive oil over medium-low heat. When the oil coats the bottom of the pan, add the onion and garlic and cook, stirring, for about 30 seconds, just until slightly softened.

2. Add the soy crumbles, raise the heat to medium-high, and cook for about 7 minutes, until the onion turns crispy. Stir in the basil, oregano, coriander, cumin, Herbamare, cayenne, and black pepper.

3. Add the beans and tomatoes, stir well, and reduce the heat to medium. Simmer for about 10 minutes, until cooked through. Serve.

Per serving: 41 grams carbohydrates, 37 grams protein, 7 grams fat

*V*egetable Side Dishes

Asparagus in Warm Tarragon Vinaigrette

While I suggest crumbled turkey bacon as a topping for this recipe, you could substitute vegetarian bacon for the same effect. What is most important about this recipe is to eat the asparagus! Full of folic acid and with significant amounts of vitamin C, thiamine, vitamin B_6, and potassium, the slender stalks are powerhouses of nutrients. In fact, in ancient times, foraging for wild asparagus was a springtime ritual—as much for the health properties of the vegetable as its delicate, distinctive, grassy flavor. Serve this with steamed fish, a salad, a glass of chilled white wine, and a piece of fruit for dessert.

Serves 6

1½ pounds asparagus
2 tablespoons balsamic vinegar
2 teaspoons Splenda
Olive oil cooking spray
1 teaspoon minced garlic
1½ teaspoons minced fresh tarragon
¾ teaspoon sea salt
⅛ teaspoon freshly ground pepper
2 tablespoons chopped toasted pecans
2 slices cooked turkey bacon, crumbled

1. Snap the tough ends off the asparagus where the spears break naturally when you bend them, and discard. Slice the spears into 1½-inch pieces.

2. In a small bowl, stir together the vinegar and Splenda.

3. Coat a large nonstick skillet well with olive oil cooking spray, and heat over medium-high heat. When the skillet is hot, add the garlic and sauté for about 1 minute, until softened but not browned. Add the asparagus and sauté for about 5 minutes, until tender.

4. Add the vinegar mixture, tarragon, salt, and pepper, and stir well. Cook for about 2 minutes, stirring, until well mixed and heated through. Sprinkle the pecans and bacon over the asparagus, and serve immediately.

Per serving: 3 grams carbohydrates, 2 grams protein, 13 grams fat

String Beans with Sesame Seeds

With just a hint of nuttiness from the sesame seeds and oil, this quick-and-easy string bean dish is terrific. I prepare it in a wok, but a large nonstick skillet will work well, too. Either way, stir it constantly as it cooks, which is only minutes, and then you're done!

Serves 4

2 teaspoons olive oil
2 garlic cloves, crushed
1 pound string beans
2 tablespoons mirin, dry white wine, or vermouth
1 tablespoon low-sodium tamari or soy sauce
2 teaspoons toasted sesame seeds (see note on page 167)
¼ teaspoon toasted sesame oil

1. Heat a nonstick wok over medium-high heat. Pour in the olive oil, and tip the wok so that the oil slides over the surface. Add the garlic

and cook, stirring, for about 30 seconds, until fragrant but not colored. If the garlic threatens to burn, reduce the heat.

2. Add the beans and stir-fry for about 4 minutes, until they begin to soften. Add the mirin, tamari, sesame seeds, and sesame oil. Mix well, and stir-fry for 1 minute, or until the beans are crisp-tender. Serve immediately.

Per serving: 7 grams carbohydrates, 0 grams protein, 4 grams fat

Steamed Summer Squash

Few recipes are as effortless as this one, and if you have a trusty steamer, you'll be tempted to make it over and over. And why not? We all should eat more vegetables, and we're always looking for ways to do so. I drizzle the squash with a little almond oil for its lovely, rich flavor, but you could substitute olive oil. Almond oil is a Zone-favorable, monounsaturated fat and is sold in the health food sections of large supermarkets and in health food stores. You can also substitute zucchini, string beans, broccoli, or another vegetable for the squash—another reason to call on this recipe regularly.

Serves 2

2 cups sliced yellow summer squash (about ½ pound)
2 teaspoons almond oil or olive oil
Herbamare and freshly ground pepper

1. Put the squash in a steaming basket and set the basket over boiling water, or put it in a steamer. Cover tightly, and steam for about 7 minutes, until the squash is tender.

2. Transfer the squash to a serving bowl, drizzle with almond oil, and season to taste with Herbamare and pepper. Serve immediately.

Per serving: 4.5 grams carbohydrates, 0 grams protein, 3 grams fat

Zucchini Boats

Ever wondered what to do with relatively large zucchini? Here's a brilliant idea: Cut the zucchini lengthwise, scrape out the seeds, and then fill the "boats" with an appealing mixture of spinach and ricotta cheese. Bake the filled zucchini for about 20 minutes. Serve this course with a simple protein such as grilled chicken or fish.

Serves 4

3 zucchini (about 1 pound), halved lengthwise and seeded
2 teaspoons olive oil
1 small yellow onion, finely chopped
1 garlic clove, minced
⅛ teaspoon freshly grated nutmeg
1 10-ounce package frozen chopped spinach, thawed and well
    drained
½ cup low-fat ricotta cheese
Juice and grated zest of ½ lemon
2 tablespoons grated Parmesan or soy Parmesan cheese

1. Preheat the oven to 375°F.

2. Arrange the zucchini halves in a single layer in a deep skillet, and add enough water to cover them. Bring the water to a boil over medium-high heat, and cook for 3 to 5 minutes, or until the zucchini

are just fork-tender. Transfer the zucchini, again in a single layer, to a shallow baking dish.

3. In the same or a clean skillet, heat the olive oil over medium-high heat. Add the onion, garlic, and nutmeg, and sauté for 3 to 4 minutes, or until the onion is tender. Adjust the heat as necessary to keep the garlic from burning. Add the spinach, ricotta, lemon juice, and lemon zest, and stir well.

4. Spoon the spinach mixture over the zucchini halves, spreading it evenly. Bake for about 20 minutes, until heated through and the filling is bubbling around the edges. Sprinkle with Parmesan and serve 1½ zucchini boats for each person.

Per serving: 4 grams carbohydrates, 5 grams protein, 2.5 grams fat

Baked Zucchini and Tomatoes

Zucchini is a wonderful squash and nearly always easy to find. I particularly like it in late summer and early fall when backyard gardeners have more than they know what to do with (hint: give it to me!) and farmers' markets sell it fresh-picked at bargain prices. I use soy cheese here to limit the amount of saturated fat, but if you prefer to use dairy cheese, make sure it's low-fat. If you have left-overs, reheat them in the microwave—it works well.

Serves 6

Olive oil cooking spray
2 teaspoons olive oil
1 leek, white part only, thinly sliced
3 6- to 7-inch-long zucchini, diced

½ cup quartered mushrooms
Herbamare
Sea salt and pepper
4 eggs
2 cups egg whites (6 or 7 whites)
2 tablespoons soy cream cheese
¼ cup coarsely chopped or shredded soy mozzarella cheese
¼ cup grated soy Parmesan cheese
2 tomatoes, thinly sliced
Fresh basil leaves

1. Preheat the oven to 350°F. Coat a 2-quart casserole with olive oil cooking spray.

2. In a nonstick skillet, heat the olive oil over medium heat. Add the leek and sauté for 1 to 2 minutes, or until it begins to soften. Add the zucchini and mushrooms, and sauté for 4 to 5 minutes, or until the vegetables begin to soften. Season to taste with Herbamare, salt, and pepper. Transfer the zucchini mixture to a colander to drain. Press gently on the vegetables to extract as much liquid as possible.

3. Meanwhile, in a food processor fitted with the metal blade, beat the eggs, egg whites, and cream cheese until smooth. Season lightly with Herbamare, salt, and pepper.

4. Pour the egg mixture evenly into the casserole. Add the drained vegetables, and top with the mozzarella and Parmesan cheeses.

5. Bake for about 30 minutes, until the eggs puff up slightly, the cheese melts, and a toothpick inserted in the center comes out clean. Pull the casserole from the oven, and lay the tomato slices and basil over the top. Return the casserole to the oven and bake for about 10 minutes longer, until the tomatoes are soft and lightly browned.

Per serving: 8 grams carbohydrates, 21 grams protein, 3.5 grams fat

Grilled Eggplant with Hoisin Sauce

Eggplant, a Zone-favorable vegetable if ever there was one, is fantastic on the grill. Here, once grilled, it's doused with a gingery sauce sweetened with fructose, spiked with hot pepper sauce and balsamic vinegar, and flavored with Asian ingredients such as mirin, tamari, hoisin sauce, and sesame oil.

Serves 2

Olive oil cooking spray
3 tablespoons hoisin sauce
2 tablespoons balsamic vinegar
2 tablespoons mirin
1½ tablespoons low-sodium tamari or soy sauce
1 tablespoon toasted sesame oil
1 teaspoon granulated or syrup fructose*
1 teaspoon hot red pepper sauce
½ tablespoon shredded fresh ginger
1 garlic clove, minced
1 large eggplant (about 2 pounds), cut crosswise and then into
    ¼-inch-thick slices
4 scallions, white and green parts, sliced diagonally
1 tablespoon toasted sesame seeds (see note on page 167)

1. Prepare a charcoal or gas grill, or preheat the broiler. Coat the grill rack with olive oil cooking spray. The coals or heating elements are ready when they are medium-hot.

2. In a mixing bowl, whisk together the hoisin sauce, vinegar, mirin, tamari, sesame oil, fructose, hot sauce, ginger, and garlic.

3. Grill or broil the eggplant slices for about 5 minutes on each side, until tender and lightly browned. Grilled slices should have defined grill marks on both sides.

4. Using tongs so that you don't puncture them, transfer the eggplant slices to a serving platter. Pour the hoisin sauce over them. Sprinkle with scallions and sesame seeds, and serve.

Per serving: 36 grams carbohydrates, 0 grams protein, 6 grams fat

*Fructose is sold in natural food stores in granulated or syrup form. It's sweeter than sugar but lower in calories. Fructose is made from fruits and honey and cannot be substituted directly for sugar (sucrose). Use only as specified in recipes (although you can use it to sweeten drinks to taste).

Zone Tip

Ginger isn't all flavor: It also has medicinal value. Studies have shown that it aids the digestive system and is beneficial if you have a cold or cough.

Spicy Eggplant Stir-Fry

Japanese eggplants, also called Asian eggplants, are smaller, slimmer, and longer than the purple globe eggplants more familiar to most Americans. They range from pale lavender to deep purple and are available in most markets. You also may encounter many other varieties of eggplant, including white, pink, and striped ones in assorted sizes. In this dish, for a little more protein, add an extra third of a cup of soy crumbles.

Serves 2

1 tablespoon olive oil

1 pound Japanese eggplants, peeled and sliced diagonally into
1-inch-thick rounds

1 red bell pepper, cut into long strips

2 garlic cloves, minced

1½ tablespoons shredded fresh ginger

2 scallions, white and green parts, finely chopped

2 cups soy crumbles

2 tablespoons low-sodium tamari or soy sauce

2 teaspoons chili paste with garlic

1 teaspoon red wine vinegar

½ teaspoon Splenda

¼ cup low-sodium chicken broth

1 teaspoon toasted sesame oil

1. Heat a wok over medium-high heat. Pour in ½ tablespoon of the
olive oil, and tip the wok so that the oil slides over the surface. Add
the eggplant and bell pepper, and cook, stirring, for about 5
minutes, until the vegetables begin to soften. Remove the vegetables
and set them aside.

2. Pour the remaining ½ tablespoon olive oil into the wok, and add
the garlic, the ginger, and half of the scallion. Reduce the heat to low
and cook, stirring, for about 30 seconds, until fragrant.

3. Add the soy crumbles, raise the heat, and stir-fry for about 1
minute, until the crumbles are hot. Add the tamari, chili paste,
vinegar, and Splenda, and stir-fry for about 30 seconds, until the
mixture begins to bubble.

4. Return the eggplant and bell pepper to the wok. Add the
remaining scallion and the chicken broth, and stir-fry over medium-
high heat for about 3 minutes, until the vegetables and seasonings
are heated through. Pour the sesame oil over the vegetables, stir
briefly, and serve.

Per serving: 16 grams carbohydrates, 21 grams protein, 10 grams fat

---

Zone Tip

Grate fresh ginger in a food processor, transfer to a small, lidded glass jar, and add enough dry sherry to cover. This will keep in the refrigerator for months and absorb subtle flavor as it does. Use this lovely, fragrant ginger in any preparation that calls for ginger.

White Beans with Spinach and Shirataki

Adjust the seasoning to make this dish as spicy as you like—maybe a little more red pepper flakes or garlic—and serve it with a simple protein such as baked chicken breasts or steamed fish. The mild white beans are the perfect match for the spinach and tomatoes and mix well with them. I discovered a new product that is a great alternative to pasta. It's a tofu noodle that tastes great with the spinach and beans.

Serves 4

2 ounces sun-dried tomatoes
12 ounces fresh spinach, cleaned
2 teaspoons olive oil
2 garlic cloves, minced
1 small red bell pepper, cut into slender 2-inch-long strips
1 cup canned navy or cannellini beans, drained
1 14-ounce can tomatoes, drained and chopped, with ¼ cup of the
   juice reserved
½ teaspoon crushed red pepper flakes

1 teaspoon Herbamare
1 teaspoon dried oregano
2 8-ounce packages tofu shirataki noodles
Sea salt and freshly ground black pepper
¼ cup grated soy or low-fat Parmesan cheese

1. Bring a small amount of water to a boil. Put the sun-dried tomatoes in a small bowl, pour enough of the water over them to cover, and soak for 20 to 30 minutes. Drain the tomatoes, and halve or quarter them if large.

2. Put the spinach in a steaming basket and set the basket over boiling water, or put it in a steamer. Cover tightly, and steam for about 3 minutes, until wilted. Drain, and squeeze out the moisture. Chop the spinach finely, and then sift through it with your fingers to separate the chopped leaves.

3. In a large nonstick skillet, heat the olive oil over medium heat. Add the garlic and bell pepper, and sauté for 2 to 3 minutes, or until the garlic is golden and the pepper strips just begin to soften.

4. Add the beans, canned tomatoes, reserved tomato juice, red pepper flakes, Herbamare, oregano, and drained sun-dried tomatoes. Stir gently to mix, and bring the liquid to a simmer.

5. Stir the spinach into the simmering liquid, and cook for about 1 minute, until hot.

6. Cook the noodles according to the package directions. Drain.

7. Transfer the contents of the skillet to a bowl. Add the noodles, toss well to combine, and season to taste with salt and black pepper. Sprinkle with Parmesan and serve.

Per serving: 17 grams carbohydrates, 3 grams protein, 3 grams fat

Brazilian Black Beans with Salsa

No fat, no protein, but what a great carbohydrate to accent broiled fish or grilled chicken! Plus, this recipe comes together with minimal time and effort. Black beans are used widely throughout Central and South America, and even in my corner of chilly New England, they are extremely popular. If you prefer to soak dry black beans and then cook them, rather than use canned, soak the beans in cold water for at least 6 hours or overnight, drain them, cover them with water, bring the water to a boil, and simmer the beans for 35 minutes to 1 hour. For more on cooking beans, turn to page 83.

Serves 4

Olive oil cooking spray
1 cup chopped yellow onion
1 green bell pepper, chopped
1 garlic clove, chopped
2 16-ounce cans black beans, drained
1 teaspoon Herbamare
Salsa-in-the-Zone, page 235

1. Coat a nonstick skillet with olive oil cooking spray, and heat it over medium heat. Put the onion, bell pepper, and garlic in the skillet, and cook for about 2 minutes, until the garlic softens.

2. Add the beans and cook, stirring frequently, for about 10 minutes, until the flavors blend and the contents are heated through. Season with Herbamare, and cook for a few more seconds.

3. Serve topped with salsa.

Per serving: 28 grams carbohydrates, 0 grams protein, 0 grams fat

Salsa-in-the-Zone

While many brands of store-bought salsa taste fine and are low in carbohydrates and fat, nothing beats homemade. I make this with canned tomatoes, which means it's doable any time of the year. Keep some in the refrigerator so that it's ready when you are, and for the best flavor, let it come to room temperature before serving.

Makes about 2½ cups

1 16-ounce can unsalted tomatoes, drained
¼ cup diced red or white onion
2 garlic cloves, minced
1 tablespoon red or white wine vinegar
1 teaspoon extra-virgin olive oil
1 tablespoon chopped fresh cilantro
3 or more dashes of hot red pepper sauce

1. In a nonreactive bowl, break up the tomatoes with a large spoon. Add the onion, garlic, vinegar, olive oil, and cilantro. Season to taste with hot sauce.

2. Cover and refrigerate for at least 2 hours. Let the salsa return to room temperature before serving.

Per 2 tablespoons: 2 grams carbohydrates, 0 grams protein, 0.5 gram fat

---

Zone Tip
Salsa is a fabulous condiment for livening up foods. Even most store-bought salsas have only 1 to 2 grams of carbohydrates per 2 tablespoons. You can doctor up commercial salsas with chopped fresh cilantro, scallion, jalapeño, or roasted bell pepper.

Steamed Butternut Squash with Bok Choy and Mushrooms

Butternut squash is at its peak in the fall, and here, the bok choy and mushrooms enhance its autumnal goodness. Peel the squash, remove the seeds, and chop the flesh. If you want, substitute another vegetable for the squash.

Serves 4

⅓ cup chopped butternut squash
3 cups chopped bok choy
1 cup halved white mushrooms
Sea salt and freshly ground pepper

1. Put the squash in a steaming basket and set the basket over boiling water, or put it in a steamer. Cover tightly, and steam for about 15 minutes, until soft.

2. Add the bok choy and mushrooms, and steam for about 5 minutes longer, until both are soft. Add more boiling water to the steamer if necessary.

3. Drain the vegetables and transfer them to a serving bowl. Season with salt and pepper to taste, and serve.

Per serving: 27 grams carbohydrates, 0 grams protein, 0 grams fat

---

Zone Tip
Just about all vegetables can be steamed:
    Broccoli: 5 minutes
    Carrots: 8 to 10 minutes
    Kale: 10 minutes
    Leeks: 3 minutes
    Parsnips: 8 to 10 minutes

Pea pods: 4 minutes
Scallions: 2 minutes
Swiss chard: 4 minutes
Zucchini and summer squashes: 6 minutes

Kale and White Bean Salad

If you're looking for ways to work more legumes into your diet, here's a lovely recipe that uses white beans but also takes advantage of kale. I discovered kale's versatility a few years ago when I started buying it from a local farmer at our farmers' market and have been hooked ever since. It wilts in minutes and tastes just great with the beans and the garlic and other seasonings. Plus, it's a good source of calcium and folic acid. Try this as an accompaniment to fish. It's fantastic!

Serves 4

2 teaspoons olive oil
1 yellow onion, chopped
1 garlic clove, chopped
1 pound fresh kale, thick stems removed, chopped into 1- to 2-inch
    pieces
1 cup chicken or vegetable broth
1 15-ounce can white or garbanzo beans, drained and rinsed
¼ teaspoon crushed red pepper flakes
Herbamare
Freshly ground black pepper
2 teaspoons fresh lemon juice

1. In a large, deep-sided skillet or saucepan, heat the olive oil over medium-low heat. Add the onion and garlic, and cook for about 5 minutes, until softened.

2. Rinse the kale in a colander under cool running water. Shake the colander, and then add the kale, with water still clinging to the leaves, to the skillet. Cook, stirring often, for about 5 minutes, until the kale wilts.

3. Add the chicken broth, beans, and red pepper flakes. Season to taste with Herbamare and black pepper, and simmer for about 10 minutes, stirring occasionally, until the kale is tender.

4. Sprinkle with lemon juice, and serve hot or at room temperature.

Per serving: 29 grams carbohydrates, 0 grams protein, 1.5 grams fat

---

Zone Tip

Bring your walking shoes to work and try to take a brisk, fifteen-minute walk during your lunch break. You will feel revitalized and be more productive for the rest of the afternoon.

Roasted Vegetable Casserole

This impressive vegetable casserole is about as "gourmet" as I get. I often make it for a dinner party, complemented by a dish such as Scallops with Orange and Sesame Oil, page 115, a green salad with Gloria's Vinaigrette, page 98, and then for dessert, some berries scattered over Microwave Apples, page 258. I adapted this from a recipe that included red bliss potatoes, sweet potatoes, and carrots, none of which are particularly Zone favorable, and so I replaced them with other vegetables. You can add your favorite veggies here, but be sure to keep the balance of high-glycemic vegetables to low-glycemic vegetables at about one to four. In my version below, the only vegetables with high-glycemic indexes are parsnips, beets, and butternut squash. Everything else is low.

Serves 4

4 small beets
About 1 tablespoon olive oil
3 to 4 leeks, cut lengthwise, root ends and tops removed
2 red onions, each cut into 6 wedges
1 butternut or delicata squash, peeled, seeded, and sliced about 1
   inch thick
Sea salt and freshly ground black pepper
Herbamare
Olive oil cooking spray
3 parsnips, peeled and cut into chunks
2 bell peppers, 1 red and 1 orange or yellow, each cut into 6 strips
2 fennel bulbs, fronds removed, cored, cut into ½-inch-wide slices
   and then halved
2 zucchini, sliced into ½-inch-wide rounds
½ pound shiitake mushrooms, stemmed, gills scraped, and sliced
   about 1 inch thick
Handful fresh thyme leaves

1. Put the beets in a steaming basket and steam, tightly covered,
over boiling water for 10 to 12 minutes, or until fork-tender. Drain
and set aside until cool enough to handle but still warm. Slip the
skins off the beets; they should come right off. Quarter each beet.

2. Preheat the oven to 400°F.

3. Pour enough olive oil into a large casserole (about 9" × 12") to
coat the bottom. Put the leeks at opposite ends of the casserole, and
then arrange the onions around the perimeter. Lay the squash slices
in the center of the casserole to fill the bottom.

4. Sprinkle salt, black pepper, and Herbamare over the vegetables,
and spritz with a little olive oil cooking spray.

5. Layer the parsnips, bell peppers, fennel, zucchini, mushrooms, and beets over the squash and onions, seasoning with salt, pepper, and Herbamare and a spritz of olive oil cooking spray. Keep making layers and seasoning them until the casserole is tightly packed.

6. Sprinkle with thyme, and cover tightly with the lid or foil. Roast for about 2 hours, lifting off the foil and basting the vegetables with the juices accumulating in the casserole. Serve hot or warm.

Per serving: 28 grams carbohydrates, 0 grams protein, 14 grams fat

Wilted Garlic Spinach

It's always magical to cook spinach: a bulky pile of leaves cooks down in no time, so that you are left with a dark green mass bursting with earthy flavor and lots of vitamins and minerals. Be sure the spinach is very clean. The packaged fresh spinach sold in supermarkets is far cleaner than the loose leaves we used to buy, but don't depend on anyone else to clean it for you. Soak the leaves in a bowl of cool water, swishing them around and changing the water once or twice, and then drain them in a colander to rid them of any residual sand or grit.

Serves 2

2 tablespoons low-sodium chicken broth
1 tablespoon low-sodium soy sauce
1 teaspoon cornstarch
½ teaspoon toasted sesame oil
Sea salt
2 teaspoons olive oil
1 tablespoon chopped garlic
1 pound fresh spinach, cleaned

1. In a small bowl, mix together the chicken broth, soy sauce, cornstarch, and sesame oil. Taste and add salt if necessary.

2. Heat a wok over medium heat. Pour in the olive oil, and tip the wok so that the oil slides over the surface. Add the garlic and cook, stirring, for about 30 seconds, until fragrant but not colored. If the garlic threatens to burn, reduce the heat.

3. Stir the chicken broth mixture again so that the cornstarch is blended. Add it to the wok and cook for about 30 seconds, until the sauce thickens.

4. Raise the heat to medium-high, add the spinach, and stir-fry for about 2 minutes, until the spinach barely wilts and is coated with the sauce. The spinach should not be overly soft and limp. Serve immediately.

Per serving: 5 grams carbohydrates, 0 grams protein, 4.5 grams fat

Whipped Cauliflower

Once you've tried this whipped cauliflower, made with soy milk and veggie soy cream cheese, you won't miss fat-laden mashed potatoes. I use the chive-flavored veggie cream cheese in this preparation to boost its oniony taste. The soy cream cheese is sold in the refrigerator section of most supermarkets with the other soy products. Because this is made primarily of cauliflower, its glycemic index is very low, so you can enjoy it to your heart's content!

Serves 4

1 head cauliflower, cut into florets (about 4 cups florets)
¼ cup soy milk or low-fat milk

2 tablespoons veggie soy cream cheese
¼ to ½ teaspoon mild chili powder
Garlic powder
Onion powder
Herbamare and freshly ground pepper

1. Put the cauliflower florets in a steaming basket and set the basket over boiling water, or put them in a steamer. Cover tightly, and steam for about 15 minutes, until tender. Drain.

2. Transfer the hot florets to a food processor fitted with the metal blade. Add the milk and cream cheese, and process until smooth.

3. Add the chili powder, and season to taste with garlic powder, onion powder, Herbamare, and pepper. Serve immediately.

Per serving: 9 grams carbohydrates, 1 gram protein, 1.5 grams fat

Lentil and Spinach Casserole

This casserole is a good source of carbohydrates when you want something robust and filling to pair with a simple protein such as broiled or pan-seared fish or chicken. To prevent the casserole from being watery, squeeze as much moisture as you can from the thawed spinach—and then spin it in a salad spinner or press it with paper towels. The melted cheese, rich lentils, and well-seasoned spinach make this a comforting, cozy dish during the bracing months of winter.

Serves 4

8 ounces dried lentils (1¼ cups)
2 10-ounce packages frozen chopped spinach, thawed

Olive oil cooking spray
2 teaspoons olive oil
1 small yellow onion, finely chopped
1 garlic clove, minced
1 red bell pepper, finely chopped
½ teaspoon dried basil
¼ to ½ teaspoon Herbamare
¼ teaspoon dried oregano
Freshly ground black pepper
¼ cup shredded soy mozzarella or low-fat mozzarella cheese

1. In a large saucepan, bring about 2 quarts of water to a boil. Add the lentils, reduce the heat, and simmer over medium-high heat for about 30 minutes or until tender. Drain.

2. Meanwhile, put the spinach in a colander and press on it with the back of a spoon to extract moisture. Finish by squeezing the spinach with your hands and then drying it with paper towels, or by spinning it in a salad spinner. The spinach should be as dry as possible.

3. Preheat the oven to 350°F. Coat an 8-inch square baking pan with olive oil cooking spray.

4. In a nonstick skillet, heat the olive oil over medium-low heat, and then tilt the pan to coat the bottom. Add the onion and garlic, and cook for 2 to 3 minutes, or until softened. Take care that the garlic does not burn. Add the bell pepper and cook for 2 to 3 minutes longer, or until softened. Stir in the basil, Herbamare, and oregano, and add black pepper to taste. Stir in the spinach and lentils. Mix well, and then transfer the contents to the baking pan and top with mozzarella.

5. Bake for about 20 minutes, until any liquid has evaporated, the cheese is melted, and the casserole is hot. Let cool for 10 minutes before serving.

Per serving: 28 grams carbohydrates, 2 grams protein, 2.5 grams fat

Oven-Roasted Orange Vegetables

The variety of vegetables in dazzling shades of orange and red make this dish fun to prepare and to serve. I'm also wild about blood orange juice, which is shockingly crimson and a little more intense than run-of-the-mill orange juice, but if you have no choice, use the everyday stuff. You could opt to marinate the veggies overnight and then grill them if the weather cooperates, instead of roasting them as instructed here. Serve this with a lean protein for lunch or dinner, or even with an omelet for breakfast.

Serves 4

3 red bell peppers, cut into ½-inch-thick rings
3 yellow bell peppers, cut into ½-inch-thick rings
2 baby eggplants, cut into ½-inch-thick rounds
2 zucchini, cut into ½-inch-thick rounds
2 summer squash, cut into ½-inch-thick rounds
2 large portobello mushrooms, stemmed, gills scraped, and cut into
    ½-inch-thick slices
1 orange-fleshed sweet potato, cut into ½-inch-thick slices
1 red onion, cut into ½-inch-thick slices
¼ cup olive oil
Juice of 1 blood orange
3 garlic cloves, minced
1 tablespoon coarse salt or sea salt

1. Preheat the oven to 400°F.

2. Put all of the vegetable slices in a roasting pan.

3. In a large measuring cup, stir together the olive oil, orange juice, garlic, and salt. Pour the mixture over the vegetables. Using a wooden spoon or your hands, mix the vegetables so that they are well coated.

4. Roast the vegetables for 1½ to 1¾ hours, stirring every 30 minutes, until completely cooked and browned. Taste, and adjust the seasoning. Serve hot or at room temperature.

Per serving: 21 grams carbohydrates, 0 grams protein, 7 grams fat

Chick-Peas with Broccoli Rabe

If you haven't tried broccoli rabe, don't wait any longer. This recipe is my top choice for preparing the mildly bitter green with undertones of sweet mustard—and I love it with arctic char, salmon, and other fish. Also called broccoli raab, rapini, or rape, it looks rather like a small, leafy head of broccoli and is available nowadays in most markets. As for the chick-peas, use organic if you can.

Serves 4

1 pound broccoli rabe, trimmed and cut into 1-inch pieces
2 teaspoons olive oil
3 garlic cloves, thinly sliced
2 cups cooked or canned chick-peas, drained
¼ teaspoon red pepper flakes
Herbamare or sea salt and freshly ground pepper

1. Fill a saucepan about halfway with water and bring it to a boil. Add the broccoli rabe and cook over medium-high heat for about 5 minutes, until almost tender. Drain well.

2. In a large nonstick frying pan, heat the olive oil over medium-low heat. When the oil coats the pan, add the garlic and cook for about 1 minute, until pale golden. Stir in the chick-peas and pepper flakes,

and add ½ cup of water. Bring the contents to a simmer and cook for 5 minutes, stirring occasionally, or until heated through.

3. Stir in the broccoli rabe and cook for about 3 minutes, stirring, until tender. Season to taste with Herbamare and serve.

Per serving: 22 grams carbohydrates, 0 grams protein, 2.5 grams fat

Cranberry Sauce

A little of this intense cranberry sauce goes a long way toward satisfying those cravings for the bright red berries in the fall when the holidays roll around. Don't think of cranberry sauce for Thanksgiving only; serve it with turkey and chicken all winter long. This recipe, which registers low on the glycemic index, can easily be doubled or halved to meet your needs.

Makes about 4½ cups

2 12-ounce bags fresh cranberries
1 10-ounce jar fruit-juice-sweetened orange marmalade
¼ cup chopped toasted walnuts
1 tablespoon honey
Splenda

1. Preheat the oven to 400°F.

2. Rinse the cranberries. Spread them with a little water clinging to them in a shallow baking pan large enough to hold them in a single layer.

3. Bake for 10 to 12 minutes, or until the cranberries pop open and appear juicy. Pull the pan from the oven, and add the marmalade, nuts, honey, and Splenda to taste. Stir gently. Return the pan to the oven, and bake for about 5 minutes longer until slightly thickened. Adjust the sweetness and serve.

Per 2 tablespoons: 12 grams carbohydrates, 0 grams protein, 1.25 grams fat

Caponata

I serve this full-bodied vegetable mélange as a side dish with a course of fish, turkey, chicken, or eggs. I've also added a few spoonfuls to an omelet and served it as a spread with pita chips or toasts. It tastes great alongside cheese, too. The ingredients list is long, and the prep work is a little time-consuming, but once you make it, you'll be glad all over!

Makes about 2 quarts

Olive oil cooking spray
1 medium eggplant
4 small zucchini
4 small yellow squashes
2 ribs celery
1 sweet onion, such as Vidalia or Maui
1 small red onion
½ large red bell pepper
½ yellow bell pepper
4 garlic cloves, crushed
¼ cup chopped black olives
¼ cup chopped green olives

¼ cup tomato paste
⅓ cup balsamic vinegar
2 tablespoons drained capers
½ tablespoon dried oregano, or 1 tablespoon fresh
Sea salt and freshly ground black pepper
½ teaspoon Herbamare

1. Preheat the oven to 400°F. Coat a large roasting pan with olive oil cooking spray.

2. Cut the eggplant, zucchini, squashes, celery, onions, and red and yellow bell peppers into ½-inch dice. Spread the vegetables in the roasting pan, and spray them with a little olive oil cooking spray. Add the garlic, and stir to mix.

3. Roast initially for 45 to 60 minutes, stirring often, or until the vegetables are fork-tender.

4. Meanwhile, in a bowl, mix together the black and green olives, tomato paste, vinegar, capers, and oregano. Season to taste with salt, black pepper, and Herbamare. Pull the pan from the oven, and add the mixture to the vegetables. Toss well. Return the pan to the oven, and roast for 40 minutes longer, or until the vegetables are tender and well flavored.

5. Serve warm, at room temperature, or chilled.

Per 2 tablespoons: 3 grams carbohydrates, 0 grams protein, 0.5 gram fat

Southwestern Salsa

This simple mixture of tomatoes, oranges, and onions flavored with cilantro is a winner with turkey, chicken, or pork. It keeps in the refrigerator for a few days, so you can spoon it onto your plate whenever your food needs a little jazzing up.

Makes about 4½ cups

6 plum tomatoes (about 1½ pounds), chopped
2 blood oranges or other oranges, peeled and chopped
½ red onion, finely chopped (about ¾ cup)
¼ cup chopped fresh cilantro
Sea salt and freshly ground pepper

1. In a nonreactive container, mix together the tomatoes, oranges, onion, and cilantro. Season to taste with salt and pepper.

2. Cover and set aside at room temperature for 2 hours, or refrigerate overnight. Taste, and adjust the seasoning if necessary. Let the salsa come to room temperature before serving.

Per 2 tablespoons: 9 grams carbohydrates, 0 grams protein, 0 grams fat

*D*esserts and Snacks

Almond Biscotti

When I discovered I was wheat intolerant, I started experimenting with other kinds of flours and came up with these tantalizing biscotti. The absence of wheat flour makes them a little more crumbly than some cookies, so take care when you cut the browned log before baking the slices. The rice flour, soy flour, and tapioca flour are stocked by health food stores and many mainstream super-markets. Because of the nuts, there is a little protein in these cookies, but consider them a carbohydrate and enjoy them after a meal in which your carb intake has been low.

About 16 biscotti

Vegetable oil cooking spray
1 cup lightly toasted slivered almonds
1 cup brown rice flour*
½ cup soy flour*
½ cup tapioca flour*
½ teaspoon baking powder
¼ teaspoon fine sea salt
¼ cup brown rice syrup or honey
¼ cup pure maple syrup
¼ cup liquid egg substitute
3 tablespoons amaretto
1 teaspoon pure vanilla extract

1. Preheat the oven to 350°F. Spray a baking sheet with vegetable oil cooking spray, or line the baking sheet with parchment paper.

2. In a mixing bowl, combine the almonds, rice flour, soy flour, tapioca flour, baking powder, and salt. Whisk several times, and make a well in the center.

3. In a small bowl, whisk together the rice syrup, maple syrup, egg substitute, amaretto, and vanilla. Pour this mixture into the well. Using a wooden spoon, mix it with the dry ingredients, working them together from the center out to the sides. The dough will be firm.

4. Turn the dough onto a lightly floured surface, and, with flour-dusted fingers, shape it into a slightly flattened log about 12″ × 3″ × 1″. Round the ends of the log, and brush the top with any of the wet ingredients clinging to the sides of the mixing bowl.

5. Bake for 25 to 30 minutes, until the log is golden brown. Remove the baking sheet from the oven, and reduce the oven temperature to 325°F.

6. Transfer the log to a cutting board. Using a serrated knife, slice the log diagonally into ¾-inch-wide sections. Arrange the slices on their sides (cut-side down) on the baking sheet.

7. Return the baking sheet to the oven. Bake for 7 minutes, and then turn the biscotti and bake for about 7 minutes longer, until lightly browned.

8. Transfer the biscotti to a wire rack to cool completely.

Per slice: 21 grams carbohydrates, 3 grams protein, 4.3 grams fat

*Brown rice flour and soy flour are sold at natural food stores and many supermarkets. They don't have much flavor, although brown rice flour has a nuttier flavor than other rice flours. Neither has gluten. Tapioca flour, also called tapioca starch, is sold in Asian markets and some supermarkets and often is used much like cornstarch to thicken preparations.

Zone Tip

Fats are not all bad and should be eaten in moderation. In fact, monounsaturated fats help our bodies. Studies have shown that in countries where the population eats a low-carbohydrate diet with monounsaturated fats, the incidence of cardiovascular disease is drastically lower than in the United States. Fats have more calories per gram than carbohydrates, but fats also will fill you up faster. Fat-free meals are less satiating and may even make us feel like eating more, not less.

Summer Fruit Crisp

After an easy summer dinner on the grill, try this warm dessert bursting with some of the best fruit of the season: blueberries, raspberries, nectarines, and peaches. Use whatever flavor of fruit concentrate you can find. You can make it ahead of time and serve it warm or at room temperature. I make this in the summertime and a similar crisp in the fall with apples. I even like it the next day for breakfast!

Serves 12

1½ cup old-fashioned rolled oats
¼ cup brown rice flour, soy flour, or whole wheat pastry flour
¼ cup chopped walnuts
1 teaspoon ground cinnamon
½ cup frozen concentrate of blueberry, raspberry, or peach juice
1¼ cups unsweetened blueberry, raspberry, or peach juice
2 pints blueberries
1 pint raspberries
4 ripe nectarines, peeled and sliced
4 ripe peaches, peeled and sliced

1. Preheat the oven to 350°F.

2. In a mixing bowl, combine the oats, rice flour, walnuts, and ½ teaspoon of the cinnamon. Add ¼ cup of the concentrate and ¼ cup of the juice, and mix well.

3. In another bowl, toss all of the berries and sliced fruit with the remaining concentrate and juice and the remaining ½ teaspoon cinnamon.

4. Spread the fruit mixture in an 8-inch square baking dish. Top evenly with the oat mixture. Cover with foil. Bake for 25 minutes, remove the foil, and bake for about 25 minutes longer, until the fruit is bubbling around the edges and the topping is crispy and golden brown.

5. Let the crisp cool in the dish for about 10 minutes before serving.

Per serving: 25 grams carbohydrates, 0 grams protein, 2 grams fat

Sweet Crisps with Ricotta and Berries

When a friend pointed out a recipe like this one in a magazine but made with brown sugar and butter, I "zoned in" on it and quickly came up with my own, Zone-friendly version. It's a marvel! Eat these crisps after a low-fat meal of low-glycemic vegetables and lean protein. You can halve the tortillas to cut the carbs, protein, and fat but retain the great flavor.

Serves 2

2 6-inch flour tortillas
Olive oil cooking spray
1½ tablespoons Splenda, plus extra for topping, if desired
⅛ teaspoon ground cinnamon, plus extra for topping if desired
½ cup skim-milk ricotta cheese
1 cup fresh raspberries, strawberries, or blueberries, or any combination of these
1 teaspoon nonalcoholic strawberry or banana flavoring

1. Preheat the oven to 375°F.

2. Stack the tortillas, and cut off the rounded edges to make two squares. Lay the squares on a baking sheet, and coat each with olive oil cooking spray.

3. In a small dish, mix together the Splenda and cinnamon, and sprinkle the mixture evenly over the tortillas. Bake for about 10 minutes, or until golden. Let the tortillas cool on the baking sheet; they will crisp up.

4. Transfer the cooled tortillas to plates, and spread half the ricotta over each square. Top each with half of the berries and a drizzle of strawberry flavoring. Sprinkle with more Splenda and cinnamon if desired. Serve immediately.

Per serving: 22 grams carbohydrates, 7 grams protein, 6 grams fat

Zone Tip

Summer is blueberry season, and the fruit is rated the number one antioxidant by the U.S. Department of Agriculture. The blue skin contains rich anthocyanins, and the flesh contains ellagic acid and resveratrol, all phytochemicals with anticancer capabilities. Other phytochemicals in blueberries, such as proanthocyanidins and tannins, may help promote urinary-tract health by blocking bacterial growth. On top of all that, they taste delicious and are low in carbohydrates.

Apple Crisp

Where I live in New England, the fall wouldn't be fall without a heavenly baked apple dessert redolent with cinnamon and walnuts. A traditional apple pie is laden with fat and sugars, but this simple crisp packs only 2 grams of fat per serving! Indulge after a meal of lean protein such as broiled chicken, steamed fish, or tofu, and a big green salad.

Serves 10

1½ cup old-fashioned rolled oats
¼ cup brown rice flour, soy flour, or whole wheat pastry flour
¼ cup chopped walnuts
1 teaspoon ground cinnamon
½ cup unsweetened frozen apple juice concentrate
1¼ cups unsweetened apple juice
1½ to 2 pounds large, firm tart apples (about 6 to 8 apples) such as
    Cortland or McIntosh, peeled and thinly sliced

1. Preheat the oven to 350°F.

2. In a mixing bowl, combine the oats, rice flour, walnuts, and ½ teaspoon of the cinnamon. Add ¼ cup of the apple juice concentrate and ¼ cup of the apple juice, and mix well.

3. In another bowl, toss the sliced apples with the remaining ½ teaspoon cinnamon, ¼ cup apple juice concentrate, and 1 cup apple juice.

4. Spread the apple mixture in an 8-inch square baking dish. Top evenly with the oat mixture. Cover with foil. Bake for 25 minutes, remove the foil, and bake for about 25 minutes longer, until the apples are bubbling around the edges and the topping is crispy and golden brown.

5. Let the crisp cool in the dish for about 10 minutes before serving.

Per serving: 19 grams carbohydrates, 0 grams protein, 2 grams fat

Microwave Apple

The microwave is eminently useful for baking fruit. Cooking an apple with a sprinkling of cinnamon takes only a few minutes, perfect for an easy dessert or quick snack. To convert this recipe to a complete Zone snack, cut back to ½ apple, and layer 1 ounce of low-fat cheddar cheese slices over the apple half during the last minute of cooking.

Serves 1

1 firm apple such as Cortland, McIntosh, Gala, or Golden Delicious
Ground cinnamon

1. Peel and quarter the apple.

2. Put the apple quarters in a small, microwave-safe dish, and sprinkle them with cinnamon. Microwave at High for about 4 minutes, until the cinnamon is melted and the apple is tender. Cool slightly before eating.

Per serving: 18 grams carbohydrates, 0 grams protein, 0 grams fat

Zone Tip
An easy way to clean your microwave is to boil a cup of water in the microwave, let it sit a few minutes with the door closed so that it steams up the sides, and then wipe the interior clean with a damp sponge.

The Best Applesauce

When my kids were small, we went apple picking every autumn and then I'd make applesauce. The house filled with glorious aromas of apples and cinnamon, and everyone felt well nurtured and comforted. I actually developed this super-easy recipe when my son was a baby and the doctor told me I could "start him on applesauce." My family has loved it ever since. I pile as many apples as I can into a large, heavy soup pot and make a lot of sauce. After they soften, I pass them through a food mill, which is easy to use and removes the apple skins at the same time. You don't have to use a food mill; mash the soft apples with a fork or potato masher—but if you do, peel and core the apples before you cook them. Here, I add some pears for interest, but you can omit them if you can't find ripe pears. I love this warm and also keep a big bowl of freshly made applesauce in the refrigerator for a few days. Watch it disappear! I apportion the rest in small containers and freeze it to enjoy for several months to come.

Makes about 12 cups

4 pounds firm tart apples (about 16 apples), such as McIntosh and
  Cortland
1 or 2 very ripe Comice or other juicy pears
About ¼ cup unsweetened apple juice or apple cider
2 cinnamon sticks
1 to 2 teaspoons ground cinnamon

1. Cut the uncored apples and pears in half.

2. Pour enough apple juice into a large, heavy pot to just cover the bottom. Add the apples and pears, cinnamon sticks, and a good sprinkling of cinnamon. Cover the pot tightly and bring the contents to a boil over medium-high heat. This should take about 3 minutes.

3. Reduce the heat to low and simmer, covered, for 2 to 3 hours, stirring and turning the fruit from the bottom to the top every so often, until the fruit is very soft. Remove and discard the cinnamon sticks.

4. Using a large food mill set over a large bowl, process the fruit. This is easiest to do in small batches. The skin and seeds will separate from the fruit as it passes through the mill. Remove and discard the skin and seeds between batches. Eat warm or refrigerate for up to 3 days, and serve cold.

Per ½-cup serving: 15 grams carbohydrate, 0 grams protein, 0 grams fat

Zone Tip

Cravings for unfavorable foods strike everyone, even those of us most firmly devoted to the Zone. Distract yourself if you feel one coming on: take a walk, call a friend, write a letter, or watch a movie. These cravings usually only last about 30 seconds, and you don't have to give in. The craving won't haunt you unless you let it!

Poached Pears

I especially like Comice pears, which I buy every chance I get from October through January, when they tend to be in the markets. For poaching, pears must be perfectly ripe so that they exude the maximum amount of juice and taste sweet and delicious. I thicken the sauce with kuzu, a natural thickening agent from Japan that must be diluted in cold water before it's added to the hot liquids. Stir it continuously once it's added until it thickens and turns the sauce translucent. If you can't track down kuzu in a health food or specialty store, substitute arrowroot, and mix it in cold water first, too.

Serves 4

⅓ cup unsweetened apple juice
2 ripe but still firm Comice, Anjou, or Bartlett pears, peeled and quartered
½ cinnamon stick
1 teaspoon kuzu (Japanese thickening agent), mixed with 2 teaspoons cold water

1. Pour the apple juice into a pan large enough to hold the pear quarters in a single layer. Arrange the pears in the pan, and tuck the cinnamon stick between two pieces of fruit near the center of the pan.

2. Bring the contents to a boil over medium-high heat, and immediately reduce the heat so that the liquid simmers. Cover the pan, and poach the pears for about 10 minutes, until they are easy to pierce with the tip of a sharp knife.

3. Using a slotted spoon, transfer the pears to a serving platter. Remove and discard the cinnamon stick.

4. Add the kuzu mixture to the poaching liquid, and stir over low heat for about 4 minutes, or until the sauce is thickened and translucent. Pour the sauce over the pears and serve.

Per serving: 14 grams carbohydrates, 0 grams protein, 0 grams fat

---

Zone Tip
If you buy ice cream or frozen yogurt at an ice-cream stand, get a child's-size portion and be sure to have protein with it, such as chopped nuts.

Summer Cherries Jubilee

Cherries are at their glorious best in the summertime, and this jubilee is a nifty way to celebrate them. A cherry pitter, which is a small and inexpensive kitchen tool, will save you a lot of time and keep your thumb from becoming red stained. If you use an alcohol-based vanilla extract, do not add it to the cottage cheese mixture but instead use it to flavor the sauce.

Serves 4

1 cup low-fat cottage cheese*
1 cup low-fat plain yogurt*
1 tablespoon Splenda
2 teaspoons nonalcoholic vanilla flavoring or pure vanilla extract
1½ cups pitted sweet cherries
½ cup cabernet sauvignon or other dry red wine
¼ cup fruit-juice-sweetened cherry spread
1 tablespoon amaretto
2 teaspoons fresh lemon juice
1 tablespoon plus 1 teaspoon slivered almonds

1. In a food processor fitted with the metal blade, combine the cottage cheese, yogurt, Splenda, and vanilla flavoring. Process until smooth.

2. Spoon the mixture into four freezer-safe dishes. Leave about ¼ inch of headroom. Freeze for 1 hour, or until almost firm.

3. Just before serving, in a small saucepan, mix together the cherries, cabernet, and cherry spread. Bring the mixture to a boil over medium-high heat. Immediately reduce the heat, and simmer for about 5 minutes, stirring frequently, until the cherries soften and begin to break apart.

4. Remove the pan from the heat, and stir in the amaretto and lemon juice.

5. Spoon the warm cherry sauce over the frozen yogurt mixture, and serve sprinkled with slivered almonds.

Per serving: 21 grams carbohydrates, 10 grams protein, 2 grams fat

*You can substitute 10 ounces of extra-firm silken tofu and ½ cup soy milk for the cottage cheese and yogurt. Increase the vanilla flavoring to 1 tablespoon.

Chocolate-Covered Strawberries

Big, juicy strawberries are wonderful; chocolate is sublime. Put them together and you have a dessert worth every dribble. Use the best bittersweet or semisweet chocolate you can find and the biggest, most beautiful strawberries with the stems attached. You can also dip other fruit, such as cubed pineapple, tangerine sections, or orange sections. Every one is a "wow!"

Serves 2

2 ounces bittersweet or semisweet chocolate (70 percent chocolate
    solids), coarsely chopped
12 large strawberries with stems, rinsed and dried

1. Line a baking sheet or tray with wax paper. In a small microwave-safe bowl, microwave the chocolate at Medium (50 or 60 percent) for 30 seconds. Stir gently, and microwave for 30 to 40 seconds longer, or until the chocolate pieces look shiny and wet. Stir until smooth and liquid.

2. Holding the stem, dip each strawberry in the chocolate and allow any excess to drip back into the container. Rest the dipped berries on the baking sheet.

3. When all are dipped, put the baking sheet in the freezer for 10 to 15 minutes, or until the chocolate hardens and sets. Serve immediately.

Per strawberry: 1 gram carbohydrates, 0 grams protein, 1.5 grams fat

Variations

Chocolate-Dipped Pineapple: Cut half a fresh pineapple into chunks. Spear each one with a small bamboo or metal skewer, and dip it in the chocolate.

Chocolate-Dipped Oranges or Tangerines: Separate the sections of 2 navel oranges or seedless tangerines. Spear each section with a small bamboo or metal skewer, and dip it in the chocolate.

Zone Tip
Once they're ripe, most fruits keep best stored in a perforated plastic bag in the refrigerator crisper drawer. Although the exceptions—avocados, bananas, citrus fruits, pineapples, and melons—can be refrigerated, their quality is best preserved if they are kept in a dark, cool place (50°F to 65°F). Wherever you keep them, check on fruits daily. When a piece shows any sign of spoilage such as mold, extreme softness, or oozing, remove it and salvage as much as you can or discard it. Spoilage is infectious and will quickly ruin surrounding fruits.

Appendix A
Food Guide

Use this guide to put together Zone-favorable snacks and meals. For a snack, take one item from the protein group, one from the carbohydrate group, and one from the fat group. For a meal, increase the amount of protein by 3, 4, or 5 times, depending on the number of grams of protein you need for the meal. For the carbohydrates, mix and match selections from the carbohydrate group to equal the right amount of carbs. For the fats, multiply by 3, 4, or 5.

I have selected foods that are the most Zone friendly and that you should eat and enjoy as you live in the Zone.

Protein: 7 grams

Bass, fresh water	1 oz.
Bass, sea	1½ oz.
Beef (range fed/game)	1 oz.
Bluefish	1½ oz.
Calamari	1½ oz.
Catfish	2 oz.
Chicken breast, deli-style	1½ oz.
Chicken breast, skinless	1 oz.
Clams	1½ oz.
Cod	1½ oz.
Cottage cheese	¼ cup
Crabmeat	1½ oz.
Egg whites	2

Haddock	1½ oz.
Halibut	1½ oz.
Lobster	1½ oz.
Mackerel	1½ oz.
Protein powder	⅓ oz.
Salmon	1½ oz.
Sardines	1 oz.
Scallops	1½ oz.
Shrimp	2 oz.
Snapper	1½ oz.
Soy burgers	½ patty
Soy hot dog	1 link
Soy sausage	1 patty
Soy sausage links	2 links
Swordfish	1½ oz.
Tofu, firm and extra firm	3 oz.
Trout	1 oz.
Tuna, canned in water	1 oz.
Tuna steak	1 oz.
Turkey, ground	1½ oz.
Turkey breast, skinless	1 oz.

Carbohydrates: 9 grams

Alfalfa sprouts	11 cups
Apple	½
Applesauce (unsweetened)	⅓ cup
Apricots	3
Artichoke	1 medium
Artichoke hearts	1½ cups
Asparagus (12 spears)	1 cup
Bamboo shoots, cut	4 cups
Barley, dry	½ tbsp.
Bean sprouts	3 cups
Beans, black	¼ cup
Beans, green or wax	1 cup
Blackberries	¾ cup

Blueberries	½ cup
Bok choy	3 cups
Boysenberries	½ cup
Broccoli	4 cups
Broccoli, cooked	3 cups
Brussels sprouts	1½ cups
Cabbage, shredded	4 cups
Cabbage, shredded, boiled	3 cups
Cauliflower	3½ cups
Cauliflower, pieces	3½ cups
Celery, sliced	2½ cups
Cherries	8 or ¾ cup
Chick-peas	¼ cup
Collard greens, chopped	2 cups
Cucumber	1½
Cucumber, sliced	4 cups
Eggplant	1½ cups
Endive, chopped	10 cups
Escarole, chopped	10 cups
Fruit cocktail	⅓ cup
Grapefruit	½
Grapes	½ cup
Green or red peppers	2½
Green pepper, chopped	2 cups
Honeydew melon, cubed	⅔ cup
Hummus	¼ cup
Kale	1½ cups
Kidney beans	¼ cup
Kiwifruit	1
Leeks	1 cup
Lemon	1
Lentils	¼ cup
Lettuce, iceberg (6" diameter)	2 heads
Lettuce, romaine, chopped	10 cups
Lime	1
Mushrooms, boiled	2 cups

Mushrooms, chopped	4 cups
Nectarine, medium	½
Okra, sliced	1 cup
Onion, chopped	1½ cups
Onions, chopped, boiled	½ cup
Orange	½
Orange, mandarin, canned	¼ cup
Peach	1
Peach, canned	½ cup
Pear	½
Plum	1
Radishes, sliced	2½ cups
Raspberries	1 cup
Salsa	½ cup
Sauerkraut	1 cup
Slow-cooking oatmeal, cooked	⅓ cup
Slow-cooking oatmeal, dry	½ oz.
Snow peas	1½ cups
Spinach, chopped	20 cups
Spinach, chopped, cooked	3½ cups
Strawberries	1 cup
Swiss chard, chopped	2 cups
Tangerine	1
Tomato	2
Tossed salad	1
Turnip greens, chopped	4 cups
Turnip, mashed	1½ cups
Yellow squash	2 cups
Zucchini, sliced	2 cups

Fat: 0.5 grams

Almond butter	⅓ tsp.
Almonds, slivered	1½ tsp.
Almonds, whole	3
Avocado	1 tbsp.
Canola oil	⅓ tsp.

Guacamole	1 tbsp.
Macadamia nuts	1 nut
Olive oil	⅓ tsp.
Olive oil/vinegar dressing (1 part/2 parts)	1 tbsp.
Olives	3
Peanut butter, natural	½ tsp.
Peanut oil	⅓ tsp.
Peanuts	6
Tahini	½ tsp.

How to Figure the 40-30-30 Balance

To understand how to get to the correct balance of 40 percent carbohydrates, 30 percent proteins, and 30 percent fat, you have to do a little simple math. It's easy. Here's the formula to apply to any meal, recipe, or combination of food:

- Multiply the number of grams of carbohydrates and protein by 4, giving you two numbers: the total of carbohydrate and protein calories.
- Multiply the number of fat grams by 9 to figure the number of fat calories.
- Add the three numbers together for the total calories.
- Divide the three individual totals by the total number of calories. These calculations will result in the percentages that give you the 40-30-30 balance.

Apply this formula to some of the recipes in the book and you will discover they fall within the Zone's all-important 40-30-30 ratio. For example, let's apply it to the Tofu Shake-Pudding on page 42.

36 grams carbohydrates × 4 = 144 calories

28 grams protein × 4 = 112 calories

12 grams fat × 9 = 108 calories

144 + 112 + 108 = 364 total calories

Now divide the preceding calories by 364:

144 ÷ 364 = 0.395 or 40% carbohydrates

112 ÷ 364 = 0.307 or 30% protein

108 ÷ 364 = 0.296 or 30% fat

Guidelines for Healthy Adults

The following tables offer general guidelines for healthy adults. If your height and level of exercise do not fit within these guidelines, please visit the ZonePerfect website at ZonePerfect.com. Calculations are estimated ranges and are rounded off because food measurements are not always exact. *Light exercise* is defined as walking for 10 to 15 minutes per day. *Moderate exercise* is defined as walking briskly for at least 1½ hours a week. Light weight training twice a week should be part of this regimen. *Active exercise* is defined as a fairly strenuous aerobic workout for more than 1½ hours a week, combined with weight training twice a week. *Very active exercise* is defined as a strenuous aerobic workout for more than 2½ hours a week, combined with weight training twice a week.

Women five feet six and shorter whose level of exercise is light to active should consume approximately 1,100 calories each day as suggested in Table 1.

Table 1 **Women 5'6" and Shorter Whose Level of Exercise Is Light to Active**

	Breakfast	Lunch	Two Snacks	Dinner	Total Calories
Carbohydrates	29 g	29 g	18 g	33 g	40%
Protein	22 g	22 g	14 g	24 g	30%
Fat	10 g	10 g	6 g	11 g	30%
Calories	294	294	182	327	1,097

Women five feet seven and taller whose level of exercise is light to active should consume approximately 1,300 calories each day as suggested in Table 2.

Table 2 **Women 5'7" and Taller Whose Level of Exercise Is Light to Active**

	Breakfast	Lunch	Two Snacks	Dinner	Total Calories
Carbohydrates	36 g	36 g	20 g	38 g	40%
Protein	28 g	28 g	15 g	28 g	30%
Fat	12 g	12 g	6 g	13 g	30%
Calories	364	364	194	381	1,303

Women five feet seven and taller whose level of exercise is very active should consume approximately 1,400 calories each day as suggested in Table 3.

Table 3 **Women 5'7" and Taller Whose Level of Exercise Is Very Active**

	Breakfast	Lunch	Two Snacks	Dinner	Total Calories
Carbohydrates	36 g	40 g	22 g	41 g	40%
Protein	28 g	30 g	17 g	31 g	30%
Fat	12 g	13 g	8 g	14 g	30%
Calories	364	397	228	414	1,403

Men five feet nine and shorter whose level of exercise is light to active should consume approximately 1,400 calories each day as suggested in Table 4.

Table 4 **Men 5'9" and Shorter Whose Level of Exercise Is Light to Active**

	Breakfast	Lunch	Two Snacks	Dinner	Total Calories
Carbohydrates	36 g	40 g	22 g	41 g	40%
Protein	28 g	30 g	17 g	31 g	30%
Fat	12 g	13 g	8 g	14 g	30%
Calories	364	397	228	414	1,403

Men five feet ten and taller whose level of exercise is light to moderate should consume approximately 1,500 calories each day as suggested in Table 5.

Table 5 **Men 5'10" and Taller Whose Level of Exercise Is Light to Moderate**

	Breakfast	Lunch	Two Snacks	Dinner	Total Calories
Carbohydrates	43 g	43 g	22 g	43 g	40%
Protein	32 g	32 g	17 g	32 g	30%
Fat	14 g	14 g	8 g	14 g	30%
Calories	426	426	228	426	1,506

Men five feet ten and taller whose level of exercise is active should consume approximately 1,700 to 1,800 calories each day as suggested in Table 6.

Table 6 **Men 5'10" and Taller Whose Level of Exercise Is Active**

	Breakfast	Lunch	Two Snacks	Dinner	Total Calories
Carbohydrates	44 g	44 g	42 g	44 g	40%
Protein	34 g	34 g	30 g	34 g	30%
Fat	15 g	15 g	14 g	14 g	30%
Calories	447	447	410	447	1,751

$\mathcal{A}$ppendix B

Converting to Metrics

Volume Measurements

U.S.	Metric
¼ teaspoon	1.25 ml
½ teaspoon	2.5 ml
¾ teaspoon	3.75 ml
1 teaspoon	5 ml
1 tablespoon	15 ml
¼ cup	62.5 ml
½ cup	125 ml
¾ cup	187.5 ml
1 cup	250 ml

Weight Measurements

U.S.	Metric
1 ounce	28.4 g
8 ounces	227.5 g
16 ounces (1 pound)	455 g

Cooking Temperatures

Celsius/Centigrade	0°C and 100°C are arbitrarily placed at the melting and boiling points, respectively, of water and are standard to the metric system.

Fahrenheit   Fahrenheit established 0°F as the stabilized
                        temperature when equal amounts of ice,
                        water, and salt are mixed.

To convert temperatures in Fahrenheit to Celsius, use this formula:

$$C = (F - 32) \times 0.5555$$

So, for example, if you are baking at 350°F and want to know that temperature in Celsius, here's the calculation:

$$C = (350 - 32) \times 0.5555 = 176.65°C$$

Index

Page numbers in *italics* refer to recipes.